*TWAYNE'S WORLD AUTHORS SERIES*

*A Survey of the World's Literature*



# SPAIN



# Juan Timoneda

*TWAS 367*

Juan Timoneda

# Juan Timoneda

By JOHN J. REYNOLDS

*St. John's University*

TWAYNE PUBLISHERS
A DIVISION OF G. K. HALL & CO., BOSTON, MASS.

Library of Congress Cataloging in Publication Data

Reynolds, John J 1924–
Juan Timoneda.

(Twayne's world authors series; TWAS 367 : Spain)
Bibliography: pp. 159–62.
Includes index.
1. Timoneda, Juan de, d. 1583.
PQ6437.T5Z86 868'.3'09 75-9837
ISBN 0-8057-6205-1

MANUFACTURED IN THE UNITED STATES OF AMERICA

# *Contents*

# *About the Author*

John J. Reynolds received his B.A., M.A., and Ph.D. degrees at the University of California in Berkeley. He completed the doctorate in 1956 under the direction of José F. Montesinos. Following four years as a teaching assistant in Berkeley, he taught for ten years at the University of Arizona in Tucson. Since 1960 Dr. Reynolds has taught graduate and undergraduate courses at St. John's University, Jamaica, New York; as a full professor of Spanish since 1966. In addition to translating a modern Italian short story for the *Arizona Quarterly* and writing reviews of Italian prose fiction for *Books Abroad*, he has published studies and reviews, mainly on Peninsular Spanish literature of the sixteenth and seventeenth centuries, in the *Bulletin of the Comediantes*, *Hispania*, *Hispanófila*, *Modern Language Notes*, *Renaissance Quarterly*, and *Romance Notes*. To the *New Catholic Encyclopedia* (McGraw-Hill, 1967) he contributed the article on Spanish Golden Age literature. In 1971, the *New York Times* published *A Directory for Spanish-Speaking New York*, a book coauthored by Professor Reynolds.

# *Preface*

Although many partial studies of Timoneda have been written and even though scattered references to his works appear constantly, there exists no book-length investigation in English or Spanish of the total work of this influential Valencian poet, playwright, raconteur, and bookseller. It is the purpose of the present monograph to fill that gap by examining for the first time all facets of his highly diversified oeuvre. Brief chapters on the historical background and biography are followed by a long discussion of his prose fiction, the best-known and most studied of the genres cultivated by Timoneda. Chapters 4 and 5 deal respectively with the author's theater and poetry. His editorial activities and his nonfictional and non-Castilian works are treated in Chapters 6, 7, and 8. A final chapter sums up his place in the history of Spanish literature.

Timoneda's writing is essentially popular and popularizing rather than erudite or original. Consequently, my emphasis throughout is on the great variety and the vitality of the themes and genres he disseminated. Due note is taken of his role in the development of the many art forms he employed but I have tried especially to suggest that the real fascination of his work emerges when it is viewed as a vast repository of thematic material. Each theme seems to have a life of its own as it travels across the centuries and from people to people and even when it is captured momentarily in a learned—and necessarily incomplete—study.

A word must be said about quoted material. With very few exceptions I have modernized the orthography of the Spanish quotations because I believe that, in studies of the present type, the original spelling would merely distract the reader. All translations, unless otherwise indicated, are my own. In rendering verse into English, I have undertaken solely to convey the meaning in a line-by-line prose translation.

In order to present—within reasonable limits—a balanced overall picture of an author who published as much as did Timoneda and about whom so many widely dispersed comments have been made it has clearly been necessary to omit many topics and references of interest. I am acutely aware, too, of a recent dictum by the present director of the Royal Spanish Academy, Dámaso Alonso, who observes that "en materias de erudición siempre queda un rabo por desollar." (This untranslatable sentence simply means that in matters of erudition there always remains something to be done.)

The preparation of this book would have been impossible without the cooperation of many libraries and their staffs. Aside from his *Patrañuelo* (Book of Stories) and the *Sobremesa* (Table Talk), many of Timoneda's works continue to be rare, even the modern reprints being available only in limited editions owned by major libraries. Equally indispensable have been the studies of numerous investigators, many of which are referred to in the Notes and References. In this connection I must observe that, as every researcher knows, it is unfortunately not always possible to verify the statements that are incorporated from others. For instance, when I attemped to confirm P. N. Dunn's description (see p. 22) of the *Cento altre novelle antiche* appended to Francesco Sansovino's extremely rare *Cento novelle scelte* (Venice, 1571), I discovered that the contents of the copy in the Houghton Library at Harvard belie the title page, for the additional stories are missing without explanation.

Of the many persons who have aided me in one way or another, I wish to thank particularly Mrs. Barbara Muller for converting my often difficult manuscript into a typescript and Mr. Charles Priolo for helping me with the proofreading. To Professor Gerald E. Wade I am grateful for his many valuable editorial suggestions.

J. J. Reynolds

*St. John's University*

# *Chronology*

1516–1556 Reign of Ferdinand and Isabella's grandson as Charles I, King of Spain; as Charles V, Holy Roman Emperor, from 1519 to 1558.

1517 Martin Luther sets in motion the Reformation.

1518–1520 (?) Birth of Juan Timoneda in Valencia, probably son of the tanner Domingo Timoneda from Alcañiz (Teruel).

1541 Timoneda, a tanner by trade, marries Isabel Juan Ferrandis. Their four children are: Vicente (date of birth and baptism unknown), Ana Magdalena (baptized in 1551), Ysabet Magdalena (baptized in 1562), and Juan Bautista (baptized in 1565).

1545–1552 Council of Trent initiates the Counter-Reformation. A second session is convened in 1562–1563.

1547 Timoneda is now a bookseller in Mayans Street, Valencia.

1553 Timoneda's earliest known publication: a poetic chapbook entitled "Danza espiritual" (Spiritual Dance).

1554 Publication of the celebrated anonymous novel *Lazarillo de Tormes.*

1556–1598 Reign of Philip II.

1558 Publication of Timoneda's *Ternario espiritual* (Spiritual Ternary) containing three one-act religious plays.

1559 Treaty of Cateau-Cambrésis (April 3) marks the zenith of Spanish power. The Inquisitor-General of Spain, Fernando de Valdés, issues his famous *Index Librorum Prohibitorum.* Publication of Timoneda's *Tres comedias,* containing the three plays *Anfitrión, Menemnos, Carmelia.*

1560 Lope de Rueda in Valencia.

1561 Publication of Timoneda's *Sarao de amor* (Soirée of Love), a poetic anthology.

1562 Earliest known edition of Timoneda's *Flor de enamorados* (Flower of Lovers), a poetic anthology.

1563 First edition of Timoneda's *Timón de tratantes* (Retailers' Guide) and of his collection of facetiae, *Alivio de caminantes* (Solace of Travelers).

1564 Publication of Timoneda's *El buen aviso y portacuentos* (Good Counsel and Portable Storybook).

1565 (?) Publication of Timoneda's *Villete de amor* (Billet-doux of Love), an anthology of poems, and of the collection of plays entitled *Turiana*.

1566 Timoneda publishes Alonso de la Vega's *Tres comedias*.

1567 Publication of Timoneda's *El patrañuelo* (Book of Stories). He also publishes in this year Juan de Vergara's *Dos coloquios pastorales* (Two Pastoral Colloquies) as well as Lope de Rueda's *Cuatro comedias y dos coloquios pastoriles* (Four Plays and Two Pastoral Colloquies).

1569 Most complete edition of Timoneda's collection of facetiae entitled *El sobremesa y alivio de caminantes* (Table Talk and Solace of Travelers).

1570 Timoneda publishes Lope de Rueda's *Registro de representantes* (Register of Actors), a collection of plays.

1573 Publication of Timoneda's *cancioneros* (songbooks) entitled *Enredo de amor* (Tangle of Love), *Guisadillo de amor* (Potpourri of Love), *El truhanesco* (The Comic One) and (?) *Dechado de colores* (Color Sampler), as well as his *romanceros* (ballad books) *Rosa de amores* (Garland of Love), *Rosa española* (Spanish Garland), *Rosa gentil* (Pagan Garland), and *Rosa real* (Royal Garland).

1575 Publication of Timoneda's [*Primer*] *ternario sacramental* ([First] Sacramental Ternary) and *Segundo ternario sacramental* (Second Sacramental Ternary), each of which contains three one-act religious plays.

1580 Miguel Cervantes in Valencia during November and part of December.

1583 Timoneda dies before September 24.

## CHAPTER 1

# *Spain and Valencia in the Sixteenth Century*

THE lifetime of Juan Timoneda (1520?–1583) coincides to a great extent with the reigns of Charles V, Holy Roman Emperor from 1519 to 1558 and ruler of Spain and her empire as Charles I from 1516 to 1556, and of his son Philip II, who died in 1598.[1] However, the Valencian bookseller was not only a subject of the immense empires ruled by these two leaders but also a citizen of the kingdom of Valencia, one of the semiautonomous divisions of the Spanish monarchy.[2] It will be useful to examine, in this brief chapter, first the imperial background, and then the local ambience of which Timoneda was a product.

As they relate—whether positively or negatively—to the imperial subject Timoneda, the major historical phenomena of the sixteenth century may be listed as: (1) exploration and colonization in the Americas, (2) Italy and the Italian Renaissance, (3) Protestantism and the Counter-Reformation, and (4) the menace of Islam.

During Timoneda's lifetime, Cortés overthrew the Aztec empire (1519–1522), thereby adding Mexico ("New Spain") to the Spanish dominions, and Pizarro added Peru by his conquest of the Inca empire (1531–1534). But these events and the concomitant exploration and colonization find only minimal reflection in Timoneda's multifaceted writing. American references are limited to a few items in his *Memoria hispanea* (Hispanic Memorandum) and three anecdotes (see below, p. 33).[3] On the other hand, the Valencian's works were a commercial success in the Indies, as has been shown by I. A. Leonard: "While Timoneda's other compilations were acceptable and brought considerable sales, the most popular, judging by recurrence on colonial lists, is the well-known *Patrañuelo*."[4] The relative absence of American themes in Timoneda may be due to the fact that the enterprise of the Indies was almost exclusively an undertaking of Castile, there being comparatively little involvement of the former Crown of Aragon to which Valencia belonged.

During the sixteenth century, the Spanish monarchs counted among their dominions several important parts of what is today Italy, namely, Sicily, Naples, Milan, and Siena. The resulting cultural interpenetration of the two great peoples has been felicitously described by Arróniz in the following terms: "The language and customs of the dominators left a permanent mark on Italy, whose generous revenge was to return in abundance the gifts received, and to extend them to the fields of music, poetry, painting, [the theater, prose fiction], and other rich fruits of the Renaissance."[5] Near the end of the first third of the century the great poet Garcilaso de la Vega (1501?–1536) successfully nationalized the Italianate meters: the hendecasyllable (eleven-syllable line) and the heptasyllable (seven-syllable line). Italian playwrights, like Lodovico Ariosto (1474–1533), were read in the original or in translation. Italian actors, starting in 1548, performed in the cities and towns of Spain until the end of the century.

Also widely read, in translation or in the original, were the Italian *novellieri,* or writers of the short novels known as *novelle.* Some of the most influential were: Giovanni Boccaccio (1313–1375), Ser Giovanni Fiorentino (second half of the fourteenth century), Masuccio Salernitano (fifteenth century), Giovanni Sabadino degli Arienti (d. 1510), Gianfrancesco Straparola (d. after 1557), Matteo Bandello (1485–1561), and Giambattista Cinzio Giraldi (1504–1573). Popular in Spain, too, were the Italian writers of facetiae, among them Poggio Bracciolini (1380–1459), Piovano Arlotto (1396–1484), and Lodovico Domenichi (1515–1564). A major beneficiary and disseminator of these writers is the subject of this book.

During the reign of Charles I, Protestantism rose and expanded outside Spain. With the accession of Philip II to the throne and with the completion of the second session of the Council of Trent (1562–1563), the movement called the Counter-Reformation or Catholic Reform took root in Spain, having as its principal aims not only to eradicate heresy but also to instruct clergy and laity in the faith and to improve the morals of both groups. Among the instruments used to accomplish one or more of these ends were the Inquisition, the *Index of Forbidden Books,*[6] and the Eucharistic pageant known as the *auto sacramental.* In the development of the latter type of play Timoneda filled an important role. To the Valencian author, Protestants ("hugonotes" or "luteranos" as he called them) were simultaneously religious heretics and political enemies of Spain.

When in 1492 Ferdinand and Isabella reconquered Granada, the last Moorish stronghold in Spain, they did not put an end to enmity between Spaniards and Moslems. Mohammedan peoples continued for many decades to be an external and internal threat to Spain. Internally, the Moslems who remained after 1492 were given the option of expulsion or conversion in 1502 (Castile) and in 1525 (Valencia). The *moriscos*, as those who chose conversion are usually called, were not, however, treated as equals by the *cristianos viejos*, or "Old Christians." In fact, the latter suspected them not only of religious insincerity but also of acting in collusion with their former coreligionists, the Barbary pirates who periodically raided the coasts of Spain. In 1568–1570, a revolt of the *moriscos* in the Alpujarra region of Granada was crushed by the king's half-brother Don John of Austria. But the *morisco* problem was not finally settled until the years 1609–1614 when this group, regarded as alien, was expelled from Spain, some 135,000 from the kingdom of Valencia alone.

Externally, clashes between Moslem and Christian were numerous. Among the best known are the following: in 1535, Charles V captured the city of Tunis but it was retaken by Moslems in 1570; in 1555, the Moslems recaptured from the Spaniards the city of Bougie (Bugía) in Algeria; in 1565, the Turks were defeated at Malta; and in 1571 Don John of Austria led the Christian forces to a major naval victory over the Turks at Lepanto. References to Moslems (*moros*, *moriscos*, Turks, etc.) and to the conflicts of Christian and Moor abound in Timoneda's writing, in fiction (prose, poetry, theater) as well as nonfiction. In contrast, there are relatively few appearances of the other group of "New Christians," those of Jewish ancestry; but see below, page 25.

As indicated at the beginning of this chapter, Timoneda was the product not only of his *patria grande*, the Spanish monarchy. He was also influenced by his local environment. His *patria chica* (hometown) was Valencia, the capital city of the kingdom of that same name, comprising the modern provinces of Valencia, Castellón, and Alicante. Along with Aragon and Catalonia, the kingdom of Valencia had made up the Crown of Aragon until the latter was absorbed into the Spanish monarchy of Charles I in 1516. Valencia, however, preserved its political identity to some extent until the eighteenth century, when its *fueros*, or privileges, were completely abolished by Philip V. One of the major steps in the process which led to the loss of Valencian identity occurred during Timoneda's lifetime. It was the revolt of the *Germanía*, or Christian brotherhood, 1521–1524, largely an uprising of the middle class against an oppressive nobility and their Moorish protégés. The movement was crushed by the aristocracy with the aid of Charles I. The resulting political castilianization of Valencia was accompanied by a similar linguistic process; as the Castilian language gained prestige, the local Catalan-Valencian[7] tongue lost it. This linguistic situation is clearly reflected in Timoneda's predominant use of Castilian rather than his native Valencian variety of the Catalan language.

In the sixteenth century the city of Valencia with a population of some 62,000 was Spain's third largest metropolis, smaller only than Seville and Granada. Just three miles from its port, known as *el Grao*, the city had a multiethnic population consisting of Spaniards from various regions, Italian and French merchants, *moriscos*, some blacks, and others. Its two leading citizens, neither one a native, were the viceroy, appointed by the king, and the archbishop, designated by the pope. The names of some of these powerful leaders appear in Timoneda's dedications and elsewhere in his writings.

Among the notable archbishops are two canonized saints: St. Tomás de Villanueva and St. Juan de Ribera, who held the see from 1544 to 1555 and from 1569 to 1611, respectively. But Valencia was not only a city of saintly prelates; it also possessed what was probably the most notorious red-light district in Spain. The "burdel de Valencia" existed from the fourteenth century to the latter half of the seventeenth.[8] It is this fact that explains Timoneda's many anecdotes about prostitutes as well as Tronchón's famous remark about Valencian harlots in *Los Menemnos* (see below, p. 95).

In conclusion, two other aspects of the Valencian environment must be noted. First, the booktrade of which our author was a part had a long tradition in his native city, one of the first books printed in Spain having been made there in 1474.[9] Printers, binders, and booksellers were numerous in the city on the Turia River ("la ciudad del Turia"), as Valencia is often called. Furthermore, the city probably had a public playhouse as early as 1566.[10]

## CHAPTER 2

# *A Biographical Sketch*

IN the majority of the documents and printed works written during the author's lifetime, his name appears as Joan (the Catalan-Valencian form of Juan or John) Timoneda, rather than "de" Timoneda as is sometimes found in more recent works. His surname—to which he often refers obliquely—is the Catalan word for "thyme patch" and is also the name of a small community and a hill in the Catalonian province of Lérida in northeast Spain. The surname is found today in the provinces that once comprised the Crown of Aragon.

Juan Timoneda belongs to that large number of writers about whose life tantalizingly little is known for certain. What few facts are documented center on his children and his books.[1] From his writings emerges the picture of a methodical, hard-working, ambitious man with a sense of humor.

It is not known when or where the author's birth took place but, according to a reasonable conjecture, he was born in Valencia between 1518 and 1520, the son of a hide-tanner named Domingo Timoneda, who in 1517 arrived in Valencia from his native Alcañiz in the Aragonese province of Teruel.[2] Juan's native tongue was the Valencian variety of the Catalan language, as he himself pointed out in the "Epistle to the Beloved Reader" in his *Patrañuelo,* and in the *Buen aviso y portacuentos* (I, no. 61); see Chapter 8.

Our author too was a tanner when in 1541 he married Isabel Juan Ferrandis, daughter of a silversmith. From contemporary records we know a few facts about the couple's four children, data that reveal the thoroughly artisan-bourgeois status of the Timoneda family. Their eldest son, whose dates of birth and baptism are unknown, was a shoemaker by trade; in 1577, he married Francisca Beneta Alós, widow of a butcher. Their eldest daughter, baptized in 1551, married Martín de Unanoa, a surgeon, in 1578. Another daughter,

Ysabet Magdalena, was baptized in 1562 and presumably died before her father for she is not mentioned in his last will (1583).

The youngest child, baptized in 1565, was Joan (Juan) Bautista. In 1580 he married Ursula Vicente Juan, the daughter of a surgeon. A silk merchant and velvet weaver by trade, Joan Bautista bought Timoneda's books from his widowed mother in 1583 and continued his father's business until at least 1612.

By 1547 official documents refer to our author as a bookseller and *former* tanner. Some six years later, in a document of 1553, Timoneda sought permission to publish a number of works—poems, plays, and "other books of various stories"—that he had "composed." And, as a matter of fact, in 1553 appeared the first known work that bears Timoneda's name as composer: the two-leaved chapbook *(pliego suelto)* "Danza espiritual de muchas mujeres señaladas de la Sagrada Escritura. Hecha en alabanza de la Sacratísima Madre de Dios. Tañida por Juan Timoneda" (Spiritual Dance of Many Notable Women of Holy Scripture. Done in Praise of the Most Holy Mother of God. Performed by Juan Timoneda). For the next thirty years—his major publications dating from the period 1558 to 1575—Timoneda was to be extremely active as a bookseller, an editor and publisher of others' works, a writer, and a folklorist *avant la lettre.* In addition, there is evidence that he was an actor, at least an occasional one.

At first blush, the transformation of a hide-tanner into an author seems quite unusual. And yet the change is inescapably logical if we consider the following facts: tanned hides were used to bind books; bookbinders were often booksellers;[3] an able bookseller with a perception of the public's tastes might reasonably be expected to edit, adapt, and create materials to satisfy those tastes. Thus, although we know nothing of Timoneda's *formal* education, we can understand how this hide-tanner became an author, especially of the type that this Valencian represents.

That Timoneda was well-to-do is evident not only from the generous dowries he provided on the occasion of his children's marriages but also from the substantial legacies recorded in his testament.

As a good Valencian, Timoneda participated in two traditional activities of that city. He speculated, possibly along with his son Juan Bautista, in the famous silk market, the Gothic edifice still known as the Silk Exchange (La Lonja de la Seda) having been built between 1483 and 1498. He was also a member of the religious

Brotherhood of Our Lady of the Holy Innocents and the Forsaken. This *cofradía*, dedicated to the Patroness of Valencia, was founded in 1409.

Timoneda's bookselling, publishing, and theatrical activities brought him in contact with many prominent nonliterary as well as literary persons. Among the latter, the most interesting are Lope de Rueda (1510?–1565) and Miguel de Cervantes (1547–1616). Timoneda's friendship with Rueda cannot be documented but it can be reasonably inferred from several facts: the Valencian's expressed admiration for the Sevillan actor and dramatist; the visits of the Sevillan to Valencia, as for instance in 1560 when he, a widower, married a Valencian widow,[4] and the posthumous publication by Timoneda of Rueda's plays in 1567 and 1570.

The case of Cervantes is more complicated. In 1580, after five years of captivity in Moslem Algiers, the future author of *Don Quijote,* upon being ransomed, landed at Denia and was in Valencia in November and early December of that year. It is generally assumed that on this occasion Cervantes met the well-known Valencian bookseller.[5] Two years later, in the third act of his play *Los baños de Argel,* Cervantes refers to the publication of Lope de Rueda's plays by Timoneda "who in age conquers Time." Again, in the great novelist's *Viaje del Parnaso* (1614) there are two references to Timoneda: in Chapter VIII, Cervantes notes that Timoneda, merely by publishing Rueda's plays, acquired eternal fame. In Chapter VII, the author of *Don Quijote,* speaking of the battle between poets and poetasters, says: "So jumbled are they, that there is no one who can / discern which is good or which is bad, / which is like Garcilaso or [which is like] Timoneda." Ruiz Morcuende concludes from these lines that Cervantes was not an admirer of Timoneda's original works.[6] On the other hand, according to Rinaldo Froldi, Cervantes, without expressing a value judgment, is merely distinguishing between the Italianizing poetic current represented by Garcilaso and the native Hispanic tradition represented by Timoneda.[7]

At the end of July, 1583, Timoneda, gravely ill, signed his last will and testament, which was officially opened and read on October 1, 1583, suggesting that the author died toward the end of September in that year. He was probably buried in the famous parish church of San Juan del Mercado as he had requested in his will. In the same month of October, the famous Inventory of Timoneda's bookshop was compiled and the contents were sold by the widow to her son

Juan Bautista, who, as has been stated, was to continue the business, until at least 1612.[8]

Four woodcuts of Timoneda have survived. The earliest is found in the *Sarao de amor* (Valencia, 1561) and is repeated in the *Buen aviso y portacuentos* (Valencia, 1564) and in the *Sobremesa y alivio de caminantes* (Valencia, 1569). This is the often-reproduced portrait showing three-quarters of the author's face looking left within a frame containing the inscription—in reversed lettering—"Ioanes Timoneda Valentinus." He appears thin-faced and large-eyed, with a good-sized aquiline nose, a full head of hair and medium beard, sideburns, and moustache. He also wears a garland of laurel. In 1566, a considerably younger-looking Timoneda appeared on the title page of his edition of the three plays of Alonso de la Vega. Salvá (no. 1465)[9] and Gallardo (no. 4200)[10] assumed that this was a picture of Alonso de la Vega, but, since the very same woodcut appears in Timoneda's *Ternario sacramental* (Valencia: Joan Navarro, 1575) above a laudatory sonnet to the author by Melchor Horta, I must conclude that it is Timoneda himself who is portrayed. In this three-quarter-face portrait, the author is looking to the right and is wearing, according to Gallardo (no. 4032), "a Milanese cap with egret plumes on the left side." A profile of the mature Timoneda looking left appears above an octave addressed to actors in the Valencian's edition of Lope de Rueda's plays entitled *Registro de representantes* (Valencia, 1570). He is wearing a cap. Still another portrait, showing a somewhat inclined, nearly full face, is on the title page of the *Timón de tratantes* (Valencia: Pedro de Huete, 1575). The author looks very old and venerable and wears a garland of laurel.

Just as this biographical sketch began with the uncertainty about Timoneda's birth date and place, so it must end with two other questions. Was Timoneda ever a printer, as suggested by the seventeenth-century investigator Onofre Esquerdo? There exists no clear evidence that he was.[11] Was Timoneda blind, as reported by Mateo Alemán in his *Ortografía castellana* (Mexico, 1609)?[12] Lacking further evidence, most investigators doubt this assertion of the author of *Guzmán de Alfarache*.

## CHAPTER 3

# *Timoneda's Prose Fiction*

UNDER this heading will be considered Timoneda's two collections of facetiae—*El sobremesa y alivio de caminantes* (Table Talk and Solace of Travelers) and *El buen aviso y portacuentos* (Good Counsel and Portable Storybook)—as well as the work for which he is probably best known today, *El patrañuelo* (Book of Stories). Before dealing with these three collections individually, it will be useful to describe them collectively. I shall therefore begin by discussing (1) the stated aim of the three collections; (2) the relationship between that aim, on the one hand, and the style as well as ubiquity of the stories, on the other hand; and (3) the concept of the facetia as I apply this term to the contents of the first two anthologies.

Collectively, perhaps the outstanding characteristic of the three works is their common social purpose: they provide the reader with a store of anecdotes and tales that can be *retold.* Timoneda's *Sobremesa*[1] makes this intention very clear, for in the sonnet that follows the title page of Part I, the personified Book warns that without experience and eloquence, the one who wishes to tell these stories will only reveal his own inadequacy, concluding "therefore let the able, prudent raconteur / take from me what may suit him/ / according to the company he is in. / In this way, he will give pleasure to every listener, / praise to my author, and to him who may read, / a desire to see me for some time." Immediately following the sonnet is Timoneda's "Epistle to the Reader" in which he declares:

> Curious reader, since hearing and seeing and reading are three principal causes—when utilized—through which man comes to acquire all knowledge, those very things have so influenced me that I decided to compose the present book called *Table Talk and Solace of Travelers,* in which are

contained diverse and comic stories, pleasant and very sententious sayings. Thus what I in several years have heard, seen, and read you will easily be able to memorize in brief form in order to be able to narrate some of the present stories. But what most matters to you and me, so that we won't be taken for dull, is that, when you are in conversation and you wish to tell some anecdote, you tell it apropos of what is being discussed. . . .

Finally, the title page of Part II reads: ". . . in which are contained very elegant sayings and wise repartees and very witty exempla [so that the reader will] know how to tell them in this pleasant way." Somewhat less explicit, but nevertheless clear, is the social intent of the collection *El buen aviso y portacuentos* (1564). In his "Epistle to the Benign Reader," which precedes Part I, Timoneda links this new work with the earlier one—and, by implication, with its purpose: "In past days I had printed the first and second parts of *Table Talk and Solace of Travelers;* and as this book has been very acceptable to many friends and lords of mine, they convinced me to have printed the present book . . . which embraces and includes excellent and very facetious sayings. . . ." Furthermore, the title of Part I explicitly reveals the nature of the work: "Book One of the *Good Counsel,* by Juan Timoneda, of Pleasant Sayings [That Are] Very Eloquent and Useful for Pleasing Conversation."

Although the tales in the *Patrañuelo* (Book of Stories, 1567) are considerably longer than the anecdotes of the two previous collections, nevertheless they too were published to be *retold.* The very subtitle declares: "First part of the *patrañas* of Juan Timoneda, in which are related admirable stories, comic tales, and delicate inventions so that the wise and discreet narrator will know how to tell them." In his "Epistle to the Beloved Reader," after explaining that "'Patrañuelo' derives from 'patraña', and 'patraña' is nothing more than a fabricated invention, so skillfully expanded and structured, that it seems to have some appearance of truth," Timoneda concludes: "And so such tales are called 'rondalles' in my native Valencian language and, in the Tuscan language, 'novelas,' which means: 'You, worker, since *no velas* [you're not doing night work], I'll keep you awake with some witty and wise stories, provided you know how to tell them as they are here narrated, so that they do not lose that notable wisdom and wit with which they were put together (composed).' " Walter Pabst, while recognizing the connection between Timoneda's *Sobremesa* and the tradition of improvised narration, sees in the final words just quoted a rejection of improvisation.[2] Such an interpretation seems to me erroneous, not only because it ignores Timoneda's subtitle to the *Patrañuelo* quoted above but also because, in my opinion, Timoneda is not requesting a word-for-word retelling; he is merely warning the storyteller not to spoil them, a possibility that could result, for example, from losing the thread of the story or from the introduction of extraneous matter—two of the narrative flaws against which preceptists like Lucas Gracián Dantisco admonish.[3]

William Nelson has underscored the tendency of Renaissance storytellers to justify their fictions by proclaiming their usefulness.[4] In the case of a consumer-oriented author like Timoneda, it seems to me that he was well aware of the market for his product. In a society such as ours that is frequently glutted with radios, movies, and television, it is difficult to appreciate the important role as social entertainment that was played in the sixteenth century by the telling of stories, anecdotes, and exchanges of repartee. In fact, these were social graces to be cultivated by the perfect gentleman and, as such, are thoroughly analyzed in Book Two of that influential sixteenth-century best-seller *The Courtier* of Baldassare Castiglione (Spanish translation by Juan Boscán; Barcelona: Pedro Mompezat, 1534). This famous translation was well known to Timoneda. Not only does it appear among the books in the Inventory of his bookshop but at least five of the anecdotes in the *Sobremesa* probably derive from it, or are at least variants of Castiglione's.

What then is the literary consequence of the fact that these three collections of stories and anecdotes were written for retelling? In the first place, I believe this phenomenon explains the fundamental characteristic of Timoneda's prose style, viz., condensation—a condensation that allowed the user to reword (hopefully without spoiling) the story or anecdote. This fundamental condensation has been described in different ways by different critics. Speaking of the *Patrañuelo*, S. H. Eoff says: "The author tells his story as briefly and quickly as possible and with little embellishment."[5] Menéndez y Pelayo observes that the anecdotes of the *Sobremesa* "are told with schematic brevity, doubtless in order that 'the discreet narrator' might be able to expand them and embellish them at will. But this very concision and simplicity does not lack grace."[6] Concerning the *Buen aviso* (Good Counsel), Rudolph Schevill says: "Perhaps the most noticeable feature of the style of this collection is the use or abuse of the present and past participles, especially in absolute clauses, and the rapid change of persons referred to, owing to an extreme condensation of language."[7] Mariano Baquero Goyanes writes about the *Patrañuelo:* "In a genre like that of the short story, a schematic presentation, the predominance of the plot line over other factors (obviously neglected by Timoneda), is no defect."[8] Also speaking of the *Patrañuelo,* Peter N. Dunn observes that this collection "reads like Sansovino's *Cento novelle antiche,* the brief outlines of stories which he appended to the later editions of his *Cento novelle.*"[9] It is interesting to note that Poggio Bracciolini (1380–1459), one of Timoneda's important forerunners in the writing of facetiae, advises those who don't approve of the style of his anecdotes to "take these fables themselves and present them and deck them out to their fancy. . . ."[10]

The fact that Timoneda—and his predecessors—urge the retelling of their tales has a second important implication. It is this fact that explains why so many of the Valencian's stories, as we shall see, appeared *before* and *after* his versions. Charles Speroni reminds us that in Italy "by [Lodovico] Domenichi's time [1515–1564] facetiae were common property; and besides, in the sixteenth century plagiarism was not considered a serious infraction of an author's rights."[11] Mariano Baquero Goyanes also underscores "the slight or nonexistent importance which the story writers of the sixteenth century give to the possibility of being accused of plagiarism, since, in their time, it seemed to be accepted that short stories were something like common property that belonged to everyone and to no one in particular" (Baquero Goyanes, p. 19).

At this point it will be convenient to mention, in general, the sources of Timoneda's prose fiction. He derives his inspiration from his own experience, from oral literature or folklore, and from Peninsular and foreign authors. Not surprisingly in a period when Italian influence was so great in all the arts, the principal foreign writers who seem to have influenced Timoneda belonged to that culture. Some of these Italian writers were listed above in Chapter 1. And yet, precisely because so many of the themes and motifs were common property and belonged to universal folklore, it is usually impossible to state categorically that a specific tale of Timoneda's derives from any one source. For this reason, in the following discussion of individual anecdotes and stories, I shall refer to earlier and later variants or analogues of Timoneda's versions rather than asserting that a given version is the source of another.

In the perennial nature and ubiquity of his themes lies the greatest fascination of Timoneda's writing. For example, in the *Sobremesa*, II, no. 51, the Valencian tells the following story:

The wife of a rustic farmer was having an affair with a lawyer, who was a friend of her husband. And the farmer one day invited the lawyer to dine with him on a pair of partridges. As the wife had roasted them, and the men did not arrive, and her appetite grew, she ate them both. When they arrived for dinner, she had no other recourse than to give her husband the knife to sharpen. While the latter was sharpening the knife, she approached the lawyer and said to him: "Leave quickly, sir, because my husband has found out about our affair and he wants to cut off both your ears. Don't you see how he's sharpening the knife?" When he then started to flee, the wife said: "Husband, your friend is carrying off the partridges." Going out to the door with the knife in his hand, the farmer said: "Friend, at least one." The lawyer replied: "Son of a bitch, neither one nor both."

A more elaborate version of this same tale appears in the August, 1974, issue of a popular American magazine "for men." Called "the tale of the two ganders," the story is retold by Jonah Craig from *The Arabian Nights*. In this version, the anatomical features threatened with excision are not ears but more private parts, thus perhaps justifying the appearance of the story in the section of the magazine entitled "Ribald Classic."[12]

Timoneda's first two collections form part of the genre called facetia, which was defined by Charles Speroni in his admirable anthology *Wit and Wisdom of the Italian Renaissance* as follows:

"The facetia of the Renaissance is, in general, a brief narrative that varies in length from a few lines to one or even two pages. Its main purpose is to entertain and excite laughter by relating a humorous occurrence that often finds its conclusion in a pungent, well-timed repartee. Most frequently, the shorter the anecdote, the sharper the wit" (Speroni, p. 3). Speroni also points out (p. 4) that "whatever its antecedents, the modern facetia begins to have its own history as a separate genre in the first half of the fifteenth century, thanks mainly—if not entirely—to the collection of facetiae assembled by Poggio Bracciolini [*Liber Facetiarum* (Book of Pleasantries)]." And the genre survives to this day. The biweekly Madrid journal entitled *La Estafeta Literaria* publishes in each issue a section called "The World of Anecdotes," which includes such examples of the genre as the following: " 'Convince yourself, friend'—said the divorced man to the enthusiastic bridegroom. 'The age of marriage arrives much before the age of loving.' "[13]

## I El sobremesa y alivio de caminantes

One of the most widely read of Timoneda's works is the collection of facetiae entitled *El sobremesa y alivio de caminantes* (Table Talk and Solace of Travelers), where the very title suggests the usefulness of the contents. From the sixteenth century alone there are some seven known editions: 1563 (Medina del Campo; Zaragoza), 1569 (Valencia), 1570 (Valencia), 1576 (Alcalá), 1577 (Antwerp), and 1596 (Sevilla). References to this work (usually titled *Alivio de caminantes)* in other Golden Age authors also attest to its immense popularity; among these authors are: Juan de Ochoa (c. 1598),[14] Francisco López de Ubeda (c. 1605),[15] Francisco Rodrigues Lobo (seventeenth century),[16] Antonio Mira de Amescua (d. 1644),[17] and Thomé Pinheiro da Veiga (d. 1656).[18] This anthology is truly a "pocket book," more so in fact than many books we today describe as such. The 1577 edition at the Library of the Hispanic Society of America, even in its modern binding, measures only 3 15/16 inches in length by 2 10/16 inches in width. The ever pragmatic bookseller provided his readers with a truly portable source of entertainment, a jestbook that could be conveniently brought out—if memory failed—to regale guests at dinner or fellow travelers, as the title advertises.

The anthology, in the version of the *Biblioteca de autores españoles* (not the best but the most accessible edition) consists of a First Part, comprising eighty-eight stories, and a Second Part, made up of seventy-three anecdotes. Preceding the first eighty-eight are twelve anecdotes attributed to a deceased author named Juan Aragonés.

In these anecdotes appear many social types, professions, and trades, including masters, servants, kings, jesters, pages, husbands, wives (faithful and faithless), cuckolds, lovers, doctors, lawyers, judges, merchants, thieves, philosophers, students, poets, rustics, farmers, soldiers, the physically handicapped, *señores de salva* (men of distinction), *caballeros, hidalgos, escuderos,* and *gentileshombres.* Conspicuously absent are ecclesiastical figures, there being only three appearances in the 161 stories: in I, 34, a priest is tricked by a thief; in I, 75, a priest uses a Catalan pun; and in II, 58, intervene a chaplain, a sacristan, and a traveler (see below). On the other hand, there are references to the other major religions that had settled in the Peninsula: I, 59, 83, and 86, and II, 35, contain allusions to Jews, while I, 76, and II, 5, refer to the Moors (see below). To be discussed in the section on the *Buen aviso* are the facetiae dealing with another ethnic group that constituted a stock comic type: the *vizcaínos*, or Basques, the examples in this collection being in I, 23; II, 26, 67, and 68. Finally, mention must be made of another "profession" whose members appear in conspicuous numbers in this collection—prostitutes, the following ten stories dealing directly or indirectly with this type of woman: I, 7, 10, 11, 12, 13, 68, 79; II, 16, 66, 72. Also present in this collection are three "autobiographical" facetiae that will be discussed in connection with the *Buen aviso*, which includes ten stories of this type.

The above characters, then, constitute one of the ingredients of Timoneda's humor. They will be found, in varying mixes, with the other traditional components, situation and language.

Since it is obviously impossible to summarize 161 anecdotes, I shall instead cite seven examples that are representative of significant categories, although I am well aware of the arbitrary nature of some of my classifications and choices.

An excellent example of humor of character is Part I, no. 69, which involves that thoroughly Hispanic comic type, the *cornudo*, or cuckold:

> A peasant had a beautiful wife, who was carrying on an affair with a servant of the house. And as her husband suspected it, she, to allay his suspicions, said to him one day: "Sir husband, you should know that because the servant has spoken to me of love and so that you may see the truth, I have promised to wait for him tonight near the door of the corral. Therefore it's best that you dress in my clothes and wait for him in that place." Having said this, she went to the servant and having told him the business, she said to him: "Take a stick and when you see him come dressed that way, hit him with the stick and say: 'So lightly you believe me, treacherous bitch? For I did this only to test you.'" In short, having gone to the spot, when the cuckold had received the blows, he said to the servant: "If you weren't so faithful as you have demonstrated, one could say of me 'cuckolded and thrashed.' " "But no," said the servant, "Rather, 'on top of horns, penance.' "

This story, in particular, was very popular; Rotunda reports versions of it in Boccaccio's *Decameron* (1348–1353), Ser Giovanni's

*Pecorone* (1378), and Sansovino's *Cento novelle scelte* (1561).[19] Timoneda himself incorporates another version of it in Scenes 5 and 6 of his *Comedia Carmelia* (or *Cornelia*). In general, the theme of the cuckold was a favorite of Spanish humorists and satirists, being found—to mention only a few instances—in Timoneda's edition of Lope de Rueda's *paso* known as *Cornudo y contento* (Cuckolded and Content) and in the Valencian's *cancioneros* (songbooks) entitled *El truhanesco* (The Comic One) and *Villete de amor* (Billet-doux of Love). It is worthy of note that Timoneda nationalizes this Italianate story by introducing into it two popular proverbial sayings: "cornudo y apaleado" ("cuckolded and thrashed") and "sobre cuernos, penitencia" ("on top of horns, penance"). The latter saying involves the widespread use of horns as a symbol of cuckolding.[20] The two sayings also exemplify the characteristic concision of Timoneda's style: the first is a variant of "tras cornudo, apaleado" and is defined by the *Diccionario de autoridades* (s.v. apaleado) as a "saying that refers to someone who, having been done one injustice or injury, suffers another greater one afterwards," while the second is explained in the *Academy Dictionary* (s.v. cuerno) as being used "when someone, after having suffered some insult or harm, is treated badly or blamed for it."

According to H. Recoules, Timoneda's anecdote inspired the seventeenth-century *entremés* entitled *El amigo verdadero.*[21]

Part I, no. 1, offers a good illustration of situational humor:

A drummer had a wife who was so contrary that he could never get her to do anything that he asked her to do. Once, on their way to a place where he was to play at a wedding, he said to his wife, who was astride a donkey and carrying the drum, as they were about to cross a river:

"Dear, sing, but don't play the drum because the donkey will be frightened."

As if he had said "play it," as soon as they were in the river, the drum sounded, the frightened donkey went to the bottom and our woman landed in the river. Despite his efforts, the husband was unable to help her. Seeing that she had drowned, he went upstream to look for her. A man who was watching asked him:

"Good man, what are you looking for?" To which he replied: "My wife, who has drowned."

"And are you looking for her in the direction that is contrary to the current?"

"Yes, sir; because my wife always went contrary to my opinions."

Rotunda (p. 193) records, in addition to Timoneda's, the following versions of this extremely popular story: Jacques de Vitry, *Exempla* (thirteenth century), Etienne de Bourbon, *Exempla* (d.ca. 1261), Poggio Bracciolini, *Liber Facetiarum* (1438–1452), and Sebastián Mey, *Fabulario* (1613). Nor did the antifeminist overtones of this tale escape the Archpriest of Talavera, for he included the story in his *Corbacho* (1498), Part II, Ch. 7, under the heading "How Woman Is Disobedient." The Dominicans Henry Kramer and James Sprenger also incorporated the story in their celebrated *Malleus Maleficarum* (Hammer of Witches; earliest edition circa 1487) in Part I, Question 6, under the heading "Why Superstition Is Chiefly Found in Women." Lope de Vega, too, used the anecdote in his play *Selvas y bosques de amor*. The story has survived as a folktale in the New World where it was found by Juan B. Rael and published in his *Spanish Tales of Colorado and New Mexico,* a large collection gathered in 1930 and 1940 in north central New Mexico and south central Colorado from storytellers, most of whom "had no academic culture, some of them being illiterate, but all of [whom] proudly continue to observe the old customs of their Spanish ancestors."[22]

Anecdote no. 68 of Part I illustrates well many stories that depend for their success on verbal humor. However, in this case as in many others, to understand the humor the reader or hearer must possess some specialized knowledge about Spanish social customs of the period. The story is as follows:

> A velvet weaver, considering himself a socially superior person ("muy hidalgo"), stopped practicing his trade, saying that he had discovered that he was a knight ("caballero"). Thus he constantly frequented the company of knights. On a certain occasion he happened to be in the home of a lady, known as doña Juana, who secretly granted her favors to her friends. When the man expressed to her his jealousy of a certain gentleman ("gentilhombre"), making many threats that he would kill him, doña Juana, to insinuate his lowly birth, said to him: "Sir, if you kill him, you won't escape being hanged." To which he replied: "Yes I will, if you ask to marry me."

The implication of doña Juana's reference to hanging is intelligible if we understand that "in the hierarchy of Spanish social distinctions, it was the privilege of a *caballero* to be beheaded, while garroting and hanging was the form of the death penalty meted out to plebeians."[23]

Baldassare Castiglione, who relates a version of this anecdote in *The Courtier*, provides an explanation of the social-climbing weaver's repartee when he comments: "You see how pungent and clever this was; because in Spain, as also in many other localities, there is the custom that when a man is led to the gallows, if a public prostitute asks him to be her husband, he is set free" (Speroni, p. 291).[24] Thus this anecdote joins the already-mentioned large number of Timoneda's stories that deal directly or indirectly with prostitution.

Verbal humor also characterizes that important group of anecdotes, numbers 24 through 73 of Part II, which *purport* to explain the origin of certain Spanish proverbial expressions. I emphasize "purport" because, contrary to the apparent belief of some,[25] Timoneda does not pretend to offer a *scientific* explanation of the origin of these sayings. He is merely using a literary artifice that had been practiced extensively by Antonio Cornazano (Cornazzano; 1429–1484) in his *Liber Proverbiorum* (1518) and by Aloise Cinzio delli Fabrizi (1450 – ca. 1526) in his *Libro della origine delli volgari proverbi* (1526). Other Italian authors who occasionally apply *a posteriori* amusing tales to proverbs are Angelo Poliziano (1454–1494), Lodovico Domenichi (1515–1564), Lodovico Guicciardini (1523–1589), and Pietro Fortini (c. 1500–c. 1562). The same device is found also in *La filosofía vulgar* (1568) of Timoneda's Sevillan contemporary Juan de Mal Lara (1525?–1571).

Timoneda's practical motivation in bringing out his three books of prose fiction has been described at the beginning of this chapter. Confirmation of this aspect in the case of these proverb-centered anecdotes can be found in a relatively little-known work of the famous Mercedarian playwright Fray Alonso Remón. In his *Entretenimientos y juegos honestos y recreaciones cristianas* (Honest Entertainments and Games, and Christian Recreations) (Madrid: Viuda de Alonso Martín [por] Lucas Ramírez, 1623), Remón entitles his Chapter 13 "Of Entertainments, Recreations and Games That Are Appropriate for Those Who Travel by Land or by Sea." To such travelers he highly recommends a game that consists in "asking why this or that was said, namely proverbial sayings, or proverbs or sententious adages, and one can bet some moderate amount on who will best succeed in answering and he who does it best, wins." He then illustrates the entertainment by telling a story that supposedly explains the origin of the saying "At times a man takes home the cause of his tears."

Following is a famous example (II, 58) of Timoneda's use of this device:

The origin of the saying: "For a good chaplain, a better sacristan."[26]

In a village a chaplain was eating a roasted squab (*palomino*) when a traveler asked to be allowed to eat with him, promising to pay for his share. Since the chaplain did not agree, the traveler ate his bread alone and then said: "You should know, reverend, whether you like it or not, we have both eaten the squab: you had the taste, I had the odor." The chaplain replied: "If that is the case, I want you to pay for your part of the squab." The other man said no, and he said yes, so they chose as judge the village sacristan who was present. The latter asked the chaplain how much the squab had cost him. When he said "medio real," he ordered the traveler to take out a *cuartillo*, which the sacristan took and sounding it on top of the table, said: "Reverend, consider yourself paid by the sound, just as he ate the smell." Then the innkeeper said to the two: "For a good chaplain, a better sacristan."

Angel González Palencia devoted a fascinating article to the study of this theme, which he chose to call "The illusion is enough."[27] In addition to Timoneda's version, he quotes the following variations of the same tale: a modern oral one from Arabic Morocco; Rabelais, *Pantagruel*, Book III, Ch. 37; *Il novellino* (*Cento novelle antiche*), no. 9; Plutarch, in the life of Demetrius Phalereus; a version from India; and a Cambodian analogue. He wisely concludes that: "It is impossible to fix the interrelationships that these versions of the same tale may have. It can be seen that the narrative has gradually spread through the world over the centuries, to the Arabic world, to Europe, where traces can still be seen in popular jokes [two of which are quoted]."

Another purported explanation of a proverbial saying is no. 57 of Part II. Though not intelligible to many English-speaking readers of today, the following story would have been understood perfectly by Shakespeare and his contemporaries who shared the Spaniards' belief that the song of the cuckoo was an allusion to cuckoldry:[28]

The origin of the saying: "For me the cuckoo sang."

Strolling on the outskirts of the city one afternoon two peaceful, honorable and good men who were on their way to pick up their wives, heard a cuckoo sing. Said one of them: "For you the cuckoo has sung, friend."—"No, for you," said the other. They quarreled so furiously over this that they went before the judge so that he might decide it. The judge seeing their foolishness had them formalize the case and after they had paid their fees, he pronounced the following sentence: "You should know, good men, that for me the cuckoo has sung; therefore, go with God."

The humor of course lies in the fact that the two husbands saw in the cuckoo's song an offensive implication of cuckoldry whereas the judge saw in it the source of the legal fees he received from the two litigants.

There is an interesting analogue of this story in the *Motti e facezie* (first edition, 1514–1516?) by Arlotto Mainardi, commonly known as Piovano Arlotto (1396–1484). Furthermore, Timoneda included in his *Buen aviso* (Part II, no. 28) another anecdote based on the offensive interpretation of the cuckoo's song.

Why this bird came to be associated with cuckoldry is explained briefly by the noted Italian writer Andrea Alciati (1492–1550) who says of it with irony: "This bird which along with its other abilities, / deposits its eggs in another's nest, / like the man who affronts the wife of another."[29] A longer, erudite discussion of the topic is offered by Rodrigo Caro (1573–1647) in his *Días geniales o lúdicros*.[30]

Another proverb-centered anecdote, Part II, no. 37, will serve to exemplify a substantial number of Timoneda's anecdotes that are scatological, that is, excremental in the broadest sense. Anecdotes of a sexual or pornographic type will be discussed in connection with the *Buen aviso*. The facetia reads as follows:

Origin of the saying: "What, are you seeking a rhyming sound for it?"

Once a page who suffered from flatulence was serving at the table of his master, and being unable to avoid it, broke wind. So that his master would not notice it, he began to twist his foot in the ground, making a noise. But his master, realizing what was happening, said to him good-humoredly: "What, are you seeking a rhyming sound for it?"[31]

Although this coarse type of humor may be offensive to some, it plays a fairly important role in Timoneda's two anthologies of facetiae. There is no point in pretending that it does not exist. Of the 161 anecdotes in the *Sobremesa*, some seven are more or less scatological: I, 62, 65, 71; II, 27, 36, 37, and 61. In the *Buen aviso*, with 170 complete facetiae, the number of more or less scatological items increases to nineteen: I, 7, 9, 24, 25, 43; II, 11, 20, 35, 36, 37, 42, 45, 46, 53, 54, 59, 60, 69, and 88. In some of these cases the excrementitious element is incidental and merely verbal, while in others the humor centers in a fundamental way on crepitation, as in the story cited above. By engaging in scatological writing, the Valencian bookseller joined the distinguished company of such predecessors as Aristophanes, Lucilius, Catullus, Martial, Juvenal, and Dante. He shares this occupation also with Rabelais, Montaigne, Shakespeare, Swift, Smollet, and Joyce, who are admiringly described as "The Great Scatologists" by Professor Theodor Rosebury.[32] A notorious American example of writing in this vein is the "1601" of Mark Twain (1835–1910). Even more recently, scatology makes a significant appearance in John Barth's *The Sot-Weed Factor* (1960), "one of the most persistently bawdy and scatological art-novels ever written in any language,"[33] as well as in a film that won the International Critics Prize at the 1973 Cannes Film Festival: Marco Ferreri's "The Grande Bouffe," in which, according to one critic, "There is a Swift-like humor in the figure of [Michel] Piccoli releasing a veritable aria of flatulence while he accompanies himself on the piano."[34] Nor is stercoraceous humor infrequent among Timoneda's fellow countrymen. Four of the practitioners of this special art published their works in the first decades of the seventeenth century: Gaspar Lucas Hidalgo, author of *Diálogos de apacible entretenimiento* (Barcelona: Sebastián de Cormellas, 1605, at the Hispanic Society of America); Miguel de Cervantes, *Don Quijote*, Part I (1605); Francisco de Quevedo, *El Buscón* (1626); and the celebrated Mercedarian, Tirso de Molina (1581?–1648), numerous plays.

As a final example of the *Sobremesa's* facetiae, Part I, no. 76, will illustrate a type of verbal humor and will also permit a comparison with an earlier version that may be Timoneda's source:

> Before the Moors of the kingdom of Valencia were baptized, a thief had stolen from a Moor of Alberique some clothing or other but he denied having done so. When the two appeared before a judge so that he might settle the case, prior to the hearing of testimony, the Moor was shouting so loud at the thief that the judge, learning who he was, said: "You are to keep quiet, dog; why the devil are you barking?" The Moor answered: "Because I see a thief."

Like several other facetiae of Timoneda, this one may derive from the previously cited *Courtier* of Castiglione, Book II, where we read: "But among other witticisms, those are pleasingly phrased that are made by taking the very words and sense of another man's ridicule and turning them against him and giving him some of his own medicine; as did a litigant who, when his adversary said to him in the judge's presence, 'Why do you bark so?' replied at once: 'Because I am beholding a thief' " (Speroni, p. 277).

Clearly Castiglione's and Timoneda's stories are essentially the same, although in the latter's version it is the judge, rather than the other litigant, who directs the insult that elicits the concluding riposte. What is striking in the Valencian's story is his imaginative and successful nationalization of the material. This he accomplishes (1) by giving the tale a specific Hispanic locale (the kingdom of Valencia and the small town of Alberique), (2) by relating the action to a given historical event (the baptism of the Moors), and (3) by taking advantage of the linguistic fact that Christians used the word "dog" to insult Moors (and vice versa).

At this juncture, before discussing Timoneda's second collection of facetiae, it will be convenient to describe the various methods used by the Valencian to nationalize part of the material in these two collections. Regardless of their manifold origins, he gives many facetiae a native flavor, whether specifically Valencian or generally Hispanic, by the use of (1) Spanish toponyms (place-names)—Valencia, Murcia, Seville, Medina del Campo, Salamanca, etc.; (2) Spanish anthroponyms (personal names)—Beltrán, Pero Díaz, Lope Hernández, Sancho, Pedro Langosta, etc.; (3) Hispanic proverbial sayings that are supposedly explained by an anecdote; (4) specific Hispanic persons—Duke of Calabria, Garci Sánchez de Badajoz, Oliver, etc.; (5) Hispanic regional types—Castilians, Valencians, Aragonese, Basques, etc.; and (6) Catalan-Valencian in *Sobremesa,* I, 6 and 75; *Buen aviso,* I, 29 and 61.

## II El buen aviso y portacuentos

Encouraged by the success of his *Sobremesa y alivio de caminantes* (1563), Timoneda brought out in the following year his second collection of facetiae, *El buen aviso y portacuentos* (Good Counsel and Portable Storybook).

Of this collection of anecdotes, there are only three known editions of the sixteenth century, all by Valencian printers: 1564, 1569, and 1570.[35] Like the *Sobremesa* it is truly a pocket book, the 1564 edition owned by the Hispanic Society measuring only 5 6/16 inches in length and 3 9/16 inches in width even in the modern binding. In view of this small size it is not surprising that only one copy of the earliest edition is known to exist.

Part I of this collection contains seventy-one stories; Part II comprises one hundred three, or ninety-nine if we exclude two that are missing and two incomplete ones. Structurally, the tales of Part I differ not only from those of Part II but also from those of the *Sobremesa* in that they all end in from three to fourteen lines of verse. The verse may contain the punch line or a summary or an explanation-commentary. Unlike the verse endings that characterize the Conde Lucanor tales of Don Juan Manuel, Timoneda's generally do not draw a moral. In other words, whereas Timoneda's verses are generally an integral, essential part of each item, Don Juan Manuel's are not.

Rudolph Schevill, who reprinted the apparently unique 1564 edition in 1911, wrote a brief introduction to the work, in which he says:

". . . an idea of the scope of his tales may be had from some of the classes of persons who appear in them. The list contains astrologers or prophets, clowns, peasants, thieves and sharpers, students, soldiers, gluttonous servants, judges, kings, gentlemen, widows, newly married couples, and misers; there are various tales dealing with women, domestic affairs, or the training of a wife; some tell of amours, while others are simply *deshonestos y mal sonantes*. . . ."[36]

In addition, the following groups are well represented in this collection: Basques, prostitutes, merchants, physicians, philosophers, musicians, and the physically handicapped.

As was true of the *Sobremesa,* ecclesiastical figures are conspicuous by their absence: in II, no. 73, which is incomplete, the sermon of a preacher plays a part in the story; in II, no. 95, a priest is tricked by a thief (cf. *Sobremesa,* I, 34). There are no references to Jews and only two to Moors (I, 50; II, 59). Like the earlier work, the collection includes many stories that directly or indirectly involve prostitution: I, 17, 18, 29, 30, 51; II, 62, 99, 102. This anthology is almost unique, however, among all the works of Timoneda that have survived, in that it contains two "American" references: I, no. 57, involves a type later known as an *indiano* ("person back from America with great wealth"); in II, no. 84, the principal characters are a Spanish captain and an "idolatrous" Indian. In *Sobremesa,* II, 66, there is reference to a "dark-skinned merchant from the Indies."

Again, in view of the impossibility of summarizing 170 facetiae, I have chosen for quotation and discussion seven stories that are (1) representative of relatively large categories, or (2) examples of an especially significant literary theme, or (3) illustrative of Timoneda's individual approach vis-à-vis his possible sources.

Probably the most interesting of the autobiographical facetiae of our author is no. 61 in Part I:

> The author was visited by a brother of his, who hadn't seen him for twenty-three years, and was married [and lived] in Bernaldos, near Segovia, and, on seeing him so well-preserved and with so few gray hairs and that he himself had more than enough of them although he was younger in years, he said: "What is this, brother? What regimen have you followed to keep yourself so young?" To which the author—in the Valencian language, because it was his native tongue—replied the following:
>
> "A measured mouth
> and a closed purse,
> a knot on the trouser's fly
> preserve life
> and make it tranquil."

The story is condensed into only two sentences. Ruiz Morcuende (pp. ix–x) attempts to use this anecdote to determine the author's age and approximate year of birth. However ingenious they may be, his calculations are not really very useful for he bases them on at least two unverified assumptions, viz. (1) that the event described took place in 1563, the date of the book's front matter, and (2) that Timoneda's younger brother married at about age twenty. Other "autobiographical" facetiae are: *Sobremesa*, I, 5, 87; II, 11; *Buen aviso*, I, 1, 29, 31, 52, 71; II, 64, 65, 66, 94, 103. In them, Timoneda refers to himself in several ways: "the author," "the author Montidea" (an anagram), "the author Diamonte" (an anagram), and in one case, simply as "I." In all cases, not surprisingly it is he who delivers the punch line or final repartee. As was noted in Chapter 2, there is reason to believe that the Valencian author performed as an actor; one piece of evidence that supports that belief is the autobiographical anecdote no. 52 in Part I of *Buen aviso*.

By far the predominant form of "ethnic" humor in both Timoneda's books of facetiae is that which relates to Basques, those proud inhabitants of the Spanish provinces of Vizcaya, Álava, and Guipúzcoa, whose traditions and non-Indo-European ancestral language differ so markedly from those of the rest of the Peninsula. The following story, II, 42, which also happens to be somewhat scatological, typifies many that highlight the incorrect syntax—roughly approximated in translation—of the Basque who is simultaneously ignorant and sly:

> A lady sent a servant of hers named Mondragón, a native of Vizcaya, to buy a partridge for her, explaining that she felt ill and that he should see to it that the bird didn't smell bad. When he had bought it, he opened its beak to see whether it smelled; seeing that it didn't, he took it home, saying: "Here good partridge, ma'm." Taking it and sniffing it underneath as is customary she noticed that the bird smelled very bad and she said to him: "This partridge stinks, Mondragón." The Vizcayan replied: "Ma'm, if smell rump that way, also living man smell and woman."

In a long study of the Basque presence in Castilian literature, Anselmo de Legarda records that this story of Timoneda's has analogues in other Spanish writers: Melchor de Santa Cruz, *Floresta española* (1574); Juan de Arguijo (1567–1623), *Cuentos;* Luis de Pinedo (sixteenth century), *Libro de chistes;* and in the famous eighteenth-century novel *Fray Gerundio* by the Jesuit Father Francisco de Isla.[37]

In whole or in part Basques contribute to the comic character of the following anecdotes of *Buen aviso:* I, 4, 7; II, 31, 32, 33, 34, 35, 36, 37, 38, 39, 40, 41, 42, 43, 44. In the earlier *Sobremesa,* the comic Basque appears only in I, 23; II, 26, 67, 68. There is a nameless comic Basque in Timoneda's play *Aurelia* (Act II) and in other sixteenth-century theatrical pieces described by Hendrix.[38] The relative abundance of Basque stories in the two books of facetiae contrasts sharply with the small number of anecdotes dealing with other ethnic groups. Turks appear in: *Sobremesa,* I, 29; II, 9; *Buen aviso,* I, 32; II, 79.[39] In the first and second cases, the Grand Turk is outwitted by a Christian; in the third story, the Grand Turk performs an act of generosity; in the fourth case, a Turkish ambassador in Valencia makes a wry comment on the laws of that place, which elicits Timoneda's observation: "Notable remark for a Moslem."

Portuguese appear in: *Sobremesa,* I, 56; *Buen aviso,* I, 4; II, 30.[40] In the first case, a Castilian outwits the Portuguese; in the second, a Basque retaliates for the trickery of a Portuguese; and the third story makes fun of the bravado of a Portuguese.

A certain salaciousness characterized many facetiae of the Italian Renaissance, as has been noted by Speroni, who observes that "there is no denying that in our genre, many of the pleasantries are bawdy by whatever standards we may wish to judge them: so much so, that both Castiglione in his *Cortegiano* and Giovanni della Casa in his *Galateo* (the book of etiquette of the Italian sixteenth century) sternly warned against indulgence in obscene anecdotes" (Speroni, p. 11). A similar bawdiness manifests itself in a number of Timoneda's stories; for example, in the well-known no. 6 of Part I:

> A certain female friend used to urge a widow to remarry. The latter replied that she would have already done so except that she was afraid of not finding a man who would be considerate of her age and condition and she added that, regarding the sexual act, she wasn't at all interested in *that*. Having found a very honest man who lacked a reproductive organ and who was happy to marry the widow, the friend came to her one day and said: "Ma'm, I've found a perfect companion for you because he completely lacks a sex organ, for it was cut off." "Oh, oh," said the widow, "I don't want a husband like that." "God help me," said the friend, "didn't you tell me that you weren't interested in *that*?" The widow answered:
>
> "I said it:
> It is true; but I prefer
> that between husband and wife
> there always be a third party
> who can restore peace to them."

Variants of this facetia appear in Poggio Bracciolini, Sabadino Degli Arienti, and Lodovico Guicciardini.[41] Other anecdotes of *Buen aviso* that might be considered sexually obscene or at least indelicate are: I, 63; II, 6, 8, 14, 16, 19, 23, 25. On the other hand, in the earlier *Sobremesa*, perhaps only three might be regarded as very indelicate: I, 59, 67, 86. Needless to say, what is obscene in sexual as well as scatological matters is largely a moot question, even in so-called post-Puritan America. It should be remembered, nevertheless, that the *Buen aviso* bears the license to print of the Holy Office of the Inquisition in Valencia, signed by Friar Miguel de Carranza, Provincial of the Carmelite Order in the kingdoms of Valencia, Aragon, and Navarre.

Along with general categories of anecdotes such as those that have been described, the *Buen aviso* also encompasses several specific tales that are thematically related to some of the most famous works in Spanish (and world) literature. One of these that is unfortunately a little too long for quotation is no. 49 of Part I in which a king, for fear of being exposed as a cuckold, claims to see a nonexistent painting. This is the story known to readers of Hans Christian Andersen (1805–1875) as "The Emperor's New Clothes." Hispanic letters offer two celebrated variants: in Don Juan Manuel's *Conde Lucanor* (1328–1335; first printed in 1575), "Concerning What Happened to a King with Tricksters Who Made a Cloth" (*enxemplo* 32), and Cervantes' *entremés* (interlude) entitled *The Marvelous Pageant* (probably 1598–1600; first printed in 1615). Schevill suggests that perhaps Cervantes "found the germ" of his interlude in Timoneda's tale.[42]

Reminiscent of the famous episode of Raquel and Vidas in the medieval epic *Poem of My Cid* is no. 26 of Part I:

> An honorable old man was very upset and sad because his son and daughter-in-law treated him badly after he had handed over to them all he owned. There came to console him another old man, his friend who was very wise, saying: "Do you want them to serve and honor you as before? Take a trunk that I have at home, fill it with sand, and tell your son that it contains certain money that has been returned to you. And at night take some of these bronze coins and count them, making a noise, so that you can be heard while you're locked in your room." No sooner said than done. Thinking that the old man had money, the son and daughter-in-law indulged him and served and honored him, placing him at the head of the table. In short, when the old man died, they found in the trunk only sand and the following couplet:
>
> By the bulk, weight, and sound
> that from you, chest, has come,
> I was honored and maintained
> and returned to my possessions.

In the medieval epic the Cid borrows from the two moneylenders leaving with them as security two chests that, instead of containing treasure as the lenders suppose, are filled with sand. In both the poem and the anecdote, the moral is the same: the end justifies the means. Rotunda (p.157) records the following analogues of Timoneda's story: Marco Cademosto (sixteenth century), Niccolò Granucci (1522–1603), Giovanni Sercambi (1347–1424), and Clemente Sánchez de Vercial (1370?–1426). Ramón Menéndez Pidal points out many analogues of the ruse of the sand-filled chest(s): Herodotus, Justinus, Pedro Alfonso, *Gesta Romanorum,* Boccaccio, and Mateo Alemán's *Guzmán de Alfarache.*[43] The great Spanish scholar also notes that, although the anonymous composer of the epic failed to record the Cid's repayment of the loan, this omission was rectified in later versions of the story.

A variation on an age-old theme succinctly expressed in the English proverb "Don't count your chickens till they're hatched" is no. 49 in Part II:

> A good man, being a hermit in a hermitage, received as an alms a small jar of honey and as honey came to be very expensive, he placed the jar on the edge of a well and contemplating he said: "I'll buy beehives and with the beehives sheep and with the sheep land and with the land I'll be a rich man and they'll speak to me of marrying and I'll marry a rich and beautiful woman, I'll be called 'sir' and I'll have children and if anyone of them misbehaves, I'll clout him on the head." At this point he raised a stick he had in his hands, like one who wanted to hit his children, and he broke the small jar, knocking it into the well. Finding himself deceived, he said: "Of me one can say: my joy in a well *(mi gozo en el pozo).*"

The variants and analogues of this story are innumerable. In Italian, Rotunda (p. 73) reports versions by Anton Francesco Doni (1513–1574) and Lodovico Domenichi (1515–1564). In Spanish the best-known versions are in *Calila y Dimna* (Ch. VIII), in Don Juan Manuel's *Conde Lucanor (enxemplo* VII), Lope de Rueda's *paso* known as *Las aceitunas* (The Olives), and "The Milkmaid" by the eighteenth-century fabulist, Félix María Samaniego. In French, La Fontaine's "La laitière et le pot au lait" is justly famous.

Noteworthy in Timoneda's version is the incorporation, at the end, of the proverb "El gozo en el pozo" (The joy in the well), which, according to the *Diccionario de autoridades,* is used to mean that something that was expected as a certainty has vanished. The Valencian author might easily have turned this into one of his "origin of the saying" anecdotes such as are found in the *Sobremesa,* II, 24 through 73.

The fifth anecdote of Part I has acquired a certain fame as a result of its relationship—whether direct or indirect—with what is perhaps the best-known play in the Spanish language: *El burlador de Sevilla,* the original play on Don Juan, by Tirso de Molina. In both drama and anecdote a crucial role is assigned to the proverbial expression "Tan largo me lo fiáis," which, in these two contexts, may be freely, but most accurately, translated as "Judgment Day is a long way off":

> One day two highwaymen stopped a poor student and seeing that he had only a piece of linen to make two shirts, they said to him: "Brother, you know that it's an act of charity to give away a shirt when one has two of them." The student replied: "Well then, let's see whether you know how to ask for it properly." One of them said, seizing him: "God help you because we don't ask, we take; give us the linen." While measuring the cloth to keep half, the student said: "All right, brothers; do whatever you like, for in the next life you'll pay for it." To this replied the thief:
>
> "Seeing, brother, that you mock
> the two of us, and in such a way
> with the linen threaten us,
> we will take it all,
> for Judgment Day is a long way off
> *(pues tan largo lo fiáis).*"

Rotunda (p. 46) records an analogue of this story in Sabadino Degli Arienti's *Le porretane* (1483), no. 7. The Italian's anecdote may possibly have inspired Timoneda's version but, if so, as he did repeatedly, the Valencian author thoroughly nationalized his source by incorporating in it the above-mentioned proverbial phrase. The latter's appositeness is clear when we consider the words of the *Academy Dictionary* (1970) concerning "Si tan largo me lo fiáis": " 'If you are giving me such a long term' is sometimes completed with 'give me what you still have': a saying with which we show distrust that what is greatly delayed will be carried out." Furthermore, others have pointed out that the saying was employed by cloth merchants.

The proverbial expression "Tan largo me lo fiáis" (or its variant "Qué largo me lo fiáis") appears some eight times in the *Burlador* (see G. E. Wade, ed., N.Y.: Scribner's, 1969, p. 190), and also occurs repeatedly in the play *Tan largo me lo fiáis,* regarded by Professor Wade and others as an earlier version of the *Burlador*.[44]

Whether or not the anecdote influenced the play(s) remains moot. In 1942 Professors Sánchez y Escribano and Fichter suggested the possibility of such an influence.[45] In 1970, on the other hand, Professor McGrady, after reexamining the question, concluded: "The only point of contact between Timoneda's story and the drama is that they both quote the same well-known proverb."[46] At any rate, the fact remains that the two authors gave to the proverbial expression an eschatological meaning, one with humorous intent, the other with a profound theological purpose.

Speaking of the Italian Renaissance, Speroni (p. 13) observes that "in the facetiae (as in the novelle and comedies of the age) peasants, women, and priests seem to bear the brunt of the barbed anecdotes." In Timoneda's two anthologies, peasants and women abound also but, as was noted above on pages 24 and 33, priests are almost totally absent, reflecting no doubt the influence of the Council of Trent (1545–1552; 1562–1563). This important difference between the post-Tridentine Valencian and his Italian predecessors—not to mention the highly anticlerical pre-Tridentine *Lazarillo de Tormes*—emerges clearly from a comparison of Part II, no. 92, and its probable source, a tale by Poggio Bracciolini. Timoneda's version reads as follows:

> Once there was a man who had a daughter who was reputed to be a virgin. She was of a very delicate constitution and when they suggested to him as a son-in-law a very robust man, he wondered to himself whether or not he should marry her to him. Finally, he came to say: "If I give her to him, woe is me, she runs the danger of dying." Then he answered: "But, what am I saying? What greater danger can she run than having given birth three times?"

Poggio's version, as translated by Speroni, says:

> A highlander from Pergola wanted to marry the young daughter of a neighbor. When he first met her, he felt that she was still too young and innocent, but her father, who was truly a foolish man, said to him: "She is more mature than you think; she has already had three children by the cleric of our parish priest."

Most striking, of course, is the removal of the anticlerical allusion. But, in addition, Timoneda has transformed the anecdote by reducing the dialogue to an interior monologue.

Along with the major categories and themes that have been described, Timoneda's two books of facetiae also include many numerically minor ones, two of which I shall mention before dealing with the critical evaluation of this genre. Five stories involve the legendary Alexander the Great, 356–323 B.C., about whom the *Standard*

*Dictionary of Folklore* (I, 35) states: "[he] . . . has been the greatest of all folklore figures over a wider area than any other comparable personage. Remodeled in the shape of the hero desired by the various peoples who interpreted the legend, he remains today historically and traditionally without a peer." Timoneda's Alexander anecdotes are *Sobremesa*, I, 52, 57; II, 17; and *Buen aviso*, I, 39; II, 24; in them, the hero appears to be witty, generous, merciful, prudent, and the possessor of a sense of humor. Finally, the theme of suicide, so controversial in other contexts, is used four times, and, in all cases, for comic purposes: *Sobremesa*, I, 4; *Buen aviso*, I, 40, 41; II, 101.

Critical reaction to Timoneda's facetiae has been scant. In his *Orígenes de la novela* (1907), Menéndez y Pelayo reveals an ambivalent attitude toward the *Sobremesa*, the only one of the two collections that he knew firsthand. After devoting several pages largely to the sources of Timoneda's anecdotes, the great polygraph comments: "In short (and in order not to become tiresome in the examination of such light and fleeting productions), the *Table Talk and Solace of Travelers* . . . is compiled from everywhere" (Menéndez y Pelayo, p. 71). On the very next page, in a footnote, he says: "I have dealt with them very rapidly. A more detailed study of them is reserved for the one who publishes the *Spanish Book of Fables or Book of Tales*, an undertaking worthy of tempting the ambition of any lover of both popular studies and those of learned tradition. There is scarcely an anecdote in the *Table Talk* that cannot give occasion to a curious note." Moreover, as was already quoted, Menéndez y Pelayo finds that the conciseness and simplicity of the anecdotes' style "is not lacking in charm" (p. 67).

Rudolph Schevill, in his reprint of the *Buen aviso* (1911), after much negative comment, sums up his attitude toward works of the genre to which Timoneda's book belongs with the words: "And so, in spite of their unoriginal features, they are genuine representatives of a popular taste in vogue for many decades, and deserve recognition in a history of the two richest centuries of Spanish literature."[47] Professor E. B. Place finds both collections "insipid," in his *Manual elemental de novelística española* (Madrid: V. Suárez, 1926), pp. 28–29. With the latter opinion I do not agree, but, since it is a matter of taste, the readers of this book who have read fifteen of the anecdotes in translation may judge for themselves. The critic who has best captured the appeal of Timoneda's two books of facetiae is Mariano Baquero Goyanes, if we merely add to the *Patrañuelo* of which he speaks, the titles of the two anthologies of anecdotes:

> For the reader of our day, so often weighed down by the sophistication of modern narrative literature, the *Patrañuelo* can constitute a pleasant surprise and an amusing experience.
>
> Perhaps it is in periods of crisis—as Ortega y Gasset pointed out so well—when one most feels the longing, the desire to flee and to take refuge in some primitive and elemental world. Perhaps the *Patrañuelo* has something of that—and hence—from its spontaneity and even from its crudeness—proceed, paradoxically, its peculiar charm and the possible attraction that it can provoke in the contemporary reader.
>
> Baquero Goyanes, (pp. 23–24.)

## III *The* Patrañuelo

Two years after the appearance of *Buen aviso,* Timoneda received ecclesiastical permission (dated September 22, 1566) to publish the most famous of his works of prose fiction: the *Patrañuelo* (Book of Stories). In the following year (1567) the first edition was printed in Valencia by the noted firm of Juan Mey. It is necessary to insist on the date of this first edition because the existence of the book has been questioned as recently as 1973,[48] although the rare volume in the National Library of Madrid was carefully described by S. H. Eoff in his University of Chicago doctoral dissertation on the *Patrañuelo* (dated June, 1929) and it was edited by F. Ruiz Morcuende for Clásicos Castellanos in 1930 as well as by Rafael Ferreres for Clásicos Castalia in 1971. The latter edition (p. [35]) even includes a photographic reproduction of the title page showing the date MDLXVII. The number of other extant sixteenth-century editions attests to the popularity of Timoneda's collection. These editions, as listed by Eoff, are, in addition to Valencia, 1567: Alcalá de Henares, 1576, two different editions; Barcelona, 1578; Bilbao, 1580; Lisboa, 1580; Sevilla, 1583; place unknown, 1586. Like Timoneda's earlier collections of facetiae, the *Patrañuelo* is a "pocket book," the Hispanic Society's copy of Alcalá, 1576, measuring, in its more modern binding, only 5 11/16 inches in length by 3 11/16 inches in width.

As was explained at the beginning of this chapter, the tales of the *Patrañuelo,* like those of the earlier *Sobremesa* and *Buen aviso,* were offered to "the wise and discreet narrator" to be retold at the opportune time. These differ, however, in being generally longer and more fully developed stories than the earlier anecdotes. Nineteen of the twenty-two range in length between three and eleven pages; two (no. 2 and no. 4) are seventeen pages long, while one (no. 11) comprises an anomalous forty-five pages (in the Clásicos Castellanos edition where the pages measure approximately 4 1/2 by 7 inches, that is, slightly smaller than duodecimo). That Timoneda did not include the stories in a frame is probably due to their proposed retellability. In addition to the latter purpose, two important facets of the author's intentions emerge from the preliminaries, viz., the stories are not necessarily either exemplary or realistic. In his "Epistle to the Beloved Reader" he states: "As the present work proposes only to provide some pastime and pleasant recreation, discreet reader, don't think that what is contained in the present work is all true, for most of it is invented and composed from our poor knowledge and low understanding and, what's more, the name of it indicates to you clearly and distinctly what it may be, because 'Patrañuelo' derives from 'patraña,' and 'patraña' is nothing more than a fabricated fiction, so skillfully expanded and structured that it seems to have some appearance of truth." Thus, while these stories are occasionally down-to-earth and even earthy like many of the facetiae, they are more generally idealistic, fantastic, and escapist. Their ingredients are those that have always characterized *popular* literature: adventure, love, mystery, heroism, deception, suspense, illicit sex, virtue, humor, surprise, revenge, broad—rather than individualized—characterization, involved action, and, last but not least, a happy ending.

The significance of this collection in the history of Spanish literature was stated long ago (1907) by Menéndez y Pelayo, and has been repeated frequently ever since: these *patrañas* form "the first Spanish collection of stories written in imitation of those of Italy, taking from the latter the plot and the principal details, but retelling them in a prose that is familiar, simple, lively, and not unpleasant" (Menéndez y Pelayo, pp. 75–76). Much has been written, and will have to be synthesized in this book, on Timoneda's sources. The data collected by the source-hunters are conflicting, however, because of the Valencian's eclectic method of borrowing, his "system of incrustation," as G. Valli calls it, whereby he adds to the original borrowed plot details from other sources.[49] In addition, most of the themes and motifs so utilized were to be found in numberless written and oral versions. The reader must bear these facts in mind when reading the discussion of sources and analogues that follows the outline of each of the twenty-two stories.

At the beginning of this chapter we saw the relationship between Timoneda's aim to provide material for retelling and his characteristically unadorned, hurriedly concise style. In the previous paragraph we saw Menéndez y Pelayo's generally favorable impression of the Valencian's prose. It will be worthwhile, before examining the stories individually and in detail, to take note of a negative view of the volume's style. The following critique is from S. Eoff's doctoral dissertation:

> In spite of the general clarity of his writing, Timoneda's sentences are carelessly and loosely constructed, a characteristic peculiar not to Timoneda alone but to many other sixteenth-century writers. . . . Often the subject shifts within a sentence or a single verb serves for more than one meaning. Ellipses are frequent. The past participle appears separated from the auxiliary, and other peculiarities occur which were less objectionable in the sixteenth century than now. The main fault of Timoneda is his complete indifference to good taste. This results in a constant repetition and a lack of variety. The phrase, *vista la presente* [immediately], for example, becomes a monotonous reverberation and sentence after sentence begins with a participle, either present or past. This has a tendency to give the *Patrañuelo* more the appearance of a syllabus or a catalogue than a work of art. (Eoff, p. 18.)

I believe that the reason for the defects noted by Professor Eoff has been explained. Even so, an understanding of their genesis does not eliminate them.

Finally, it must be noted that each *patraña* is preceded by a *redondilla* ("an octosyllabic quatrain rhyming *a b b a* in consonance") in which Timoneda summarizes the action to follow. No doubt the author was aware that his necessarily rather enigmatic verse synopses would stimulate the reader to seek clarification in the story itself. In other words, the *redondillas* function something like movie previews or trailers. Eoff (p. 163) believes that "Timoneda is possibly following the Italians in stating a brief summary of his story at the beginning." Clemente Sánchez de Vercial (d. 1434?) included two-lined verse summaries at the beginning of the stories in his *Libro de los exemplos por a.b.c.* (composed between 1400 and 1421). Timoneda's practice here differs from that of his *Buen aviso*, Part I, and also from that of Don Juan Manuel's

*Conde Lucanor:* in the former, the verse is normally at the end and constitutes an integral part of the story; in the latter, the verse is also at the end and, rather than merely summarizing the action, it points up the moral.

In treating the twenty-two individual *patrañas*, I shall summarize each, discuss its source or sources according to the often conflicting opinions of the investigators, and mention analogues.

In the matter of sources, I shall rely heavily on the previously mentioned dissertation of Sherman Eoff, an important study that has been generally neglected by researchers in this field.

*Patraña* I

Centering on a supposedly incestuous relationship, the plot of this first story is as follows:

In Alexandria, two friends and business associates, Cosme Alejandrino and Marco César, have sons, both of whom are named Tolomeo. Cosme also has a daughter, Argentina. When Marco suffers a financial crisis, he takes his son and moves to Athens. However, Pantana, the nursemaid of the two boys, has secretly switched the look-alike children. She hopes that the still prosperous Cosme will care for Marco's son—even when he discovers his real identity—as well as his own son.

Pantana runs away from home with a young man and is later robbed and abandoned by him. She becomes a hermit under the name Fray Guillermo.

Argentina is made pregnant by her supposed brother, Tolomeo.

In the end, Fray Guillermo confesses to being Pantana and reveals that Argentina's son is not the child of her brother but of Marco's son, Tolomeo. To everyone's delight, Argentina and Tolomeo marry.

This first *patraña* concludes with the words: "Of the preceding story there exists a play entitled *Tolomea*."[50] Timoneda refers to the play of this title which was written by Alonso de la Vega and published by Timoneda himself in the very year 1566 in which he received the ecclesiastical permit to publish the *Patrañuelo*. Both Menéndez y Pelayo[51] and Sherman Eoff (pp. 51–54) have compared the two works in question but they have arrived at somewhat different conclusions regarding their relationship. The former, while recognizing even verbal similarities, believes that both Timoneda and Alonso de la Vega drew upon a common source, probably an Italian story, as yet unidentified. On the other hand, Eoff sees no need to suppose any model for the Valencian's story other than the play, although, as the American scholar indicates, Timoneda introduces some more or less significant changes.

Menéndez y Pelayo observed that Timoneda's *patraña*, "although very extravagant, does not go beyond the limits of reality."[52] In this connection a word must be said about an important motif in this and other tales of the Valencian, viz., the mistaken identity of look-alikes. Popular, and even abused, in universal oral and written literature, the phenomenon has a firm basis in reality as some recent headlines from the *New York Times* attest: "Victim in Triple Mistaken-Identity Case Absolved After 15 Months" (January 11, 1974), "Auxiliary Policeman Is Freed, 'Look-Alike' Held in Sex Case" (October 24, 1973), and "Reforms Advised in Police Line-Ups" (September 16, 1973), the reforms being recommended as a result of a case involving a falsely accused assistant district attorney and a look-alike.

*Patraña* II

Just as Menéndez y Pelayo found "repugnant"[53] the false incest theme in the first *patraña*, so contemporary readers in the age of women's liberation will be repelled by the second *patraña*, which tells the very famous story of patient Griselida (i.e., Griselda):

The vassals of the Italian Marquis Valtero urge him to marry so that he may not die without an heir, lest they be left without a lord. He promises to do so, on the condition that they must accept whomever he chooses, to which they readily agree. The Marquis marries the beautiful and virtuous shepherdess Griselida, after receiving her solemn promise to always obey him and never contradict his wishes. To test her, the Marquis has a nurse secretly substitute a dead baby for their two-month-old daughter. The latter is sent to the Count of Bononia to be cared for. He then tells Griselida that, following their daughter's death, his vassals are displeased with her on account of her humble origins. Griselida endures all without complaint. Twelve years later, Griselida gives birth to a son who, on Valtero's orders, is also secretly taken to the Count of Bononia for rearing. The Marquis now compels Griselida to endure another severe test: she must allow herself to be taken for a certain dead servant and thereafter she must play the role of servant. He then tells her that, in deference to his vassals' wishes, he will marry the young daughter of the Count of Bononia. When the latter arrives along with her small brother, she is served patiently by Griselida.

Seeing his wife's extraordinary forbearance, the Marquis finally reveals to her and all that the young girl and her brother are her children. "Thereafter husband and wife lived many years in great peace and harmony."

It is generally agreed that Timoneda's version of this "delicious although somewhat improbable tale" (Menéndez y Pelayo, p. 6) derives from Petrarch's Latin adaptation of Boccaccio's *novella* on the subject (*Decameron,* X, 10); see the studies of C. B. Bourland,[54] Menéndez y Pelayo (III, 80), and S. Eoff (pp. 54–59). In turn, "the source of Boccaccio's *Griselda* is probably an oral tale," according to a recent study by W. E. Bettridge and F. L. Utley.[55]

The story of patient Griselda seems to have appealed to our forefathers as much as it repels the modern reader; witness a few more of the famous versions in several languages: Chaucer (c. 1340–1400), *Canterbury Tales* ("Clerk's Tale"); Lope de Vega (1562–1635), *El ejemplo de casadas y prueba de la paciencia* (a play); Thomas Dekker (1570?–1641?), *Patient Grissill* (a play); Charles Perrault (1628–1703), *Grisélidis* (a tale); Gerhart Hauptmann (1862–1946), *Griselda* (a drama).

Moreover, as Menéndez y Pelayo points out (p. 12), Durán's *Romancero* includes three popular ballads on this subject, and in Lope's time, Griselda's story appeared on playing cards in France and in Castile.

Timoneda's *patraña* was one of the sources used by the little-known playwright Navarro to compose his *Comedia muy ejemplar de la marquesa de Saluzia, llamada Griselda,* printed in 1603.

### *Patraña* III

In sharp contrast to patient Griselda's behavior, Timoneda's third *patraña* shows at the end another type of wifely conduct:

In Paris, the almoner Esbarroya greatly importunes Patricia, his next-door neighbor's wife. Patricia so informs her husband, Tiberio, who orders her to invite the almoner to a tryst. When the latter appears in their house one night, Tiberio strikes him a fatal blow, and then seats the body in the outhouse of the almonry. Later that same night another almoner, supposing that Esbarroya is delaying his departure from the outhouse because of a quarrel between them, hits him on the head with a rock. The almoner, thinking he has killed Esbarroya, deposits the body at Tiberio's door. Before dawn, Tiberio finds the body and hastily places it along with a couched lance on a stallion belonging to the almonry. He then ties the animal in front of the almoners' house. Early that same morning the almoner who thinks he killed Esbarroya sets out to leave the city on a mare in heat. The stallion senses the mare, frees himself, and hotly pursues her. There is a commotion. The almoner is taken before the judge and then jailed for the murder of Esbarroya. His shock is so great that he has to be released on bail to be cared for in the almonry. One day Tiberio and Patricia quarrel. He slaps her and she shouts that he murdered Esbarroya. Tiberio is tried, condemned to death, and the innocent almoner is freed.

The first story of *Il novellino* by Masuccio Salernitano (fifteenth century) is usually regarded as the source of this *patraña*, although significant differences have been noted: among them, the fact that Masuccio's protagonist is a Spanish friar whereas Timoneda's is a Parisian almoner. Eoff (pp. 59–66), while recognizing the possible influence of Masuccio, stresses the many modifications that could have come from oral tradition, the peregrination of a corpse being a well-known folk motif that has been studied by Archer Taylor ("Dane Hew, Munk of Leicestre," *Modern Philology,* 15 [1917], 29–54).

Alberto Sánchez has pointed out that the final episode of the *patraña* bears a strong resemblance to Timoneda's *Sobremesa,* I, 20, in which a vindictive wife brings about the punishment of her husband who had murdered a neighbor.[56]

*Patraña* IV

The fourth story is unique in that it is the only one that has been translated into English. It will be noted also that the wife, Enea Sabelina, is no Griselda:

Timoneda begins by explaining that to understand this story set in ancient Rome, one must be acquainted with the Stone of Truth: by virtue of a demon within it, the mouth of this stone head, half lion and half man, snaps shut on the hand of the guilty while leaving the innocent free.

Enea Sabelina, wife of Captain Cepión Torcato, becomes involved in an affair with the physician Arsenio Rufo during the absence of her husband. Informed by his relatives of their suspicions, the captain returns to Rome. He suggests to Enea that she submit to the test of the Stone of Truth. She consults with Arsenio, who seeks the advice of the sorcerer Padulio. The latter obtains the following plan from a demon named Zelbi: on the way to the test, Enea will fall and then complain of a thorn in her foot. Arsenio, disguised as a rude peasant, will remove the thorn. Enea will then be able to swear that no man, other than her husband, has touched her except the peasant who removed the thorn. The plan is carried out; Enea passes the test. Her husband departs and is killed in battle. The doctor and Enea then marry. Statues were built after their deaths in honor of the four: Arsenio, Enea, Padulio, and Cepión Torcato.

No single source has been discovered for this tale that illustrates well how Timoneda was not concerned with the exemplary character of his stories as had been so many of his predecessors and as would be so many of his followers. Eoff (pp. 66–71) examines many of the variants of this *patraña,* which range from Sanskrit to medieval legends about Virgil and to Renaissance Italian versions, concluding that "it is likely that Timoneda recounted current oral tradition in his story and followed no written source" (p. 69). Ferreres, however, supposes that the tale must derive from some Italian novelist, "given the number of details it gives about Rome and the knowledge it shows of the Eternal City."[57]

As in other writings of this author and his contemporaries, magic and diabolical intervention play a significant role. Amid the current revival of such themes, Timoneda's use of them may not seem so antiquated as might once have been the case.

### *Patraña* V

In his fifth narrative, Timoneda returns to the incest theme, this time real and resulting in the protagonist's being simultaneously the son, nephew, and husband (almost) of a queen:

Fabela, daughter of the King of Palinodia, is pregnant by her brother Fabio. Repentant, the latter departs to seek a pardon from the pope. When it is reported that Fabio has perished during a storm at sea, Fabela decides to have her newborn son placed in a box with a golden plaque and cast into the sea by her seneschal. The box reaches an island. Here the child is baptized by the Abbot Gregorio and given the name Gregorio. The youth becomes an accomplished knight. Wearing the golden plaque, he takes leave of the Abbot and helps Queen Fabela defeat the besieging Prince of Burgundy. As a reward for his efforts, Gregorio marries Fabela. On the wedding night, Fabela, seeing the golden plaque, tells Gregorio that he is her son and nephew and now her husband, although the latter is impossible. Fabela calls on the seneschal's widow to explain the story. The Queen then suggests that all be kept secret and that Gregorio and the widow marry. They do so; Fabela takes a vow of chastity and all "lived very honorably for many happy, prosperous years in the service of God."

It is generally accepted that this *patraña,* except for its conclusion, is based upon the legendary life of Pope St. Gregory the Great as related in the influential fourteenth-century collection entitled *Gesta Romanorum* (Ch. 81).[58] In the latter version, the marriage of mother and son is consummated. Eoff notes that the differing conclusion "illustrates the common usage with Timoneda of diverging in a particular point from a source which he otherwise follows closely" (p. 73).

The legend of St. Gregory, whose origins seem to go back to the story of Oedipus and Jocasta in Greek mythology, appears in medieval French, German, and English versions as well as in the tragedy *The Mysterious Mother* by the eighteenth-century Englishman Horace Walpole.

*Patraña* VI

In his sixth *patraña,* Timoneda combines three widely diffused folk motifs:

One morning an earth-carrier finds a bag of money in the street. Later, as he and his wife are counting the gold coins, one of them falls behind a box without their noticing it. When the merchant who lost the one hundred coins offers a reward of ten, the earth-carrier turns them over to the *alcalde* who, after the necessary formalities, gives them to the merchant. The latter, upon counting them, points out that there are ninety-nine, not one hundred. The *alcalde* then declares that they must not be the merchant's and therefore are to be returned to the finder. On his way home, the latter encounters a water-carrier friend of his. When he attempts to help the friend extricate his donkey from some mud, the animal's tail comes off in his hands. The earth-carrier, forced to flee from the enraged water-carrier, bumps into a pregnant woman; he falls and is seized by a policeman. The woman has a miscarriage.

The earth-carrier is taken before the *alcalde* to answer the complaints of the water-carrier and of the husband whose wife had miscarried. The *alcalde* decides that the earth-carrier may use the donkey until its tail grows back and that he may take the woman and return her pregnant provided his wife is agreeable. But the earth-carrier's wife will not permit the other woman to enter her house.

Some days later the merchant obtains the return of his money, which is now reduced to eighty pieces. The water-carrier too decides that he will be satisfied with the tailless donkey. In the end the earth-carrier is twenty ducats richer and free of complainants.

Although examined and reexamined by investigators, the question of this *patraña's* source(s) remains unsolved. A brief chronology of the principal conflicting views will serve to show how controversial the problem is. In 1851, Liebrecht suggested the *novella* IV of Giovanni Sercambi (1347–1424).[59] In 1872 Salvá reported that an anonymous annotator had suggested Pedro Alfonso's *Disciplina Clericalis*.[60] In 1907, Menéndez y Pelayo (p. 91), rejecting Sercambi because the latter's work was not printed until the nineteenth century, cautiously proposed the ninth *novella* of the first decade of the *Ecatommiti* by Giraldi (1504–1573). In 1929, Eoff stated that "it is possible that Timoneda used the *Novella di Bussotto* as his source" (p. 78) but later declared that "Timoneda may have followed some sixteenth-century Italian *novella* yet unknown or, which is more likely, he may have told his story from current oral sources" (p. 79). In 1946, Valli rejected both Sercambi and Giraldi, indicating, however, that "it will be more fruitful, then, to seek the origin of this *patraña* in one of the sources that Alessandro d'Ancona in his learned note points out for the *novella* IV of Sercambi (Sercambi, Giovanni, *Novelle*, Bologna, 1871, p. 274)."[61]

In 1951, Gasparetti concluded a long study with the following statement: "In conclusion, though not excluding the possibility that Sercambi's *novella* [IV] might have been known to Timoneda through oral tradition, such a possibility we regard as considerably greater in the case of Sacchetti's *novella* CXCVI, which, in our view, ought to be considered much more than the other as the primary source of *patraña* VI."[62] The most recent study of this subject, that of Enrico Cerulli, appeared in 1955.[63]

According to Cerulli, this *patraña*, combining the three motifs of "the lost purse," "the aborted woman," and "the horse without a tail," is derived from the fourth *novella* of Giovanni Sercambi. Although Sercambi's stories were not printed until the nineteenth century, Cerulli[64] refers to a versified adaptation of the *novella* in question; it was printed around 1550 and contains exactly the same three episodes found in Timoneda. This is the same work that Eoff refers to as the *Novella di Bussotto*.

As Cerulli shows, the first motif, "the lost purse," has an especially interesting history. Translated from the Arabic, the tale entered Western Europe in the twelfth century in the *Disciplina Clericalis* of Pedro Alfonso. In addition to the many versions (in Latin, French, English, German, and Italian) that derive directly or indirectly from Pedro Alfonso, there is a medieval Persian analogue, in which the judge is the son of Genghis Khan, as well as a nineteenth-century version in Amharic.

The second and third motifs are also regarded by Cerulli as being of Arabic origin, the evidence for the second being at present more clear than for the third.

There are interesting analogues of Timoneda's *patraña* VI in two of Spain's most celebrated authors of the early decades of the seventeenth century: Cervantes (1547–1616) and Lope de Vega (1562–1635). The latter's play *Lo que hay que fiar del mundo*, dated "probably *ca.* 1610," includes in its second act a scene that involves "the lost purse" motif. In this case, the wisdom of Leandro resolves the argument between the two Moors Zayde and Feniso over a purse lost by the former and found by the latter.

According to Gallardo,[65] the "tailless donkey" motif may have suggested to Cervantes the episode of his exemplary novel *La ilustre fregona* (1613) in which "Lope Asturiano" (i.e., Don Diego de Carriazo) avoids losing his donkey in a card game by claiming that he bet the animal's four quarters but not the tail. Lope's demand for the tail makes him the target of much joking.

The judgments of Timoneda's *alcalde* may have inspired in a general way the equally shrewd judgments of Sancho Panza in Barataria *(Don Quijote,* Part II, Ch. 45). Rodríguez Marín, in discussing possible antecedents for Sancho's sentences, does not cite this *patraña* but he does refer to a putative folktale whose existence is inferred from this *patraña* of Timoneda's and from a sixteenth-century Portuguese literary version.[66]

*Patraña* VII

Like the first *patraña*, the seventh tells the same story as one of Alonso de la Vega's plays edited by Timoneda:

On the advice of her father, the daughter of the King of Denmark marries the Duque de la Rosa, who is ugly but rich, instead of the Conde de Astre, who is handsome but not so rich. Accompanied by Palestino, her husband's majordomo, and Apiano, her own *camarero,* the new Duquesa, disguised as a pilgrim, sets out for the shrine of Santiago de Compostela with the secret intention of getting a look at the Conde. After an innocent meeting with him she returns home where Palestino, upon seeing his amorous attentions rejected by the Duquesa, sets a trap in which he kills his own brother to make the Duquesa look guilty to the Duque. After determining her innocence by disguising himself as a confessor, the Conde de Astre joins a companion and, their identities unknown, the two engage in combat for her honor with the Duque and Palestino. The Duque is killed by the Conde's companion, and Palestino, at the point of death, confesses his treachery. The Duque's vassals make known that they would like the unknown knight who defeated Palestino to marry the Duquesa and become their lord. The Conde reveals himself and, with the approval of the King of Denmark, marries the widowed Duquesa and becomes Duque de la Rosa.

This *patraña* concludes with the declaration: "Of the preceding tale there exists a play called *La Duquesa de la Rosa.*" The latter play is one of the three by Alonso de la Vega published by Timoneda in 1566. It is generally agreed (Menéndez y Pelayo, Menéndez Pidal, Eoff, Valli, Arróniz)[67] that both the play and the *patraña* strongly resemble *novella* 44 of the second part of Bandello (1554), but the exact relationship among the three works is viewed differently by the investigators. In his 1905 essay, Menéndez y Pelayo was quite certain that both Alonso de la Vega and Timoneda based their respective works on the Bandello story. In his *Orígenes de la novela* (1907), however, he recognized the validity of his great disciple Menéndez Pidal's suggestion that there might have been an intermediate text between the Italian author and the two Spaniards (Menéndez y Pelayo, p. 85). On the other hand, Eoff, after examining the many possibilities and their relationships, concludes that "Timoneda's story seems to be a combination of two influences [Bandello and Alonso de la Vega] rather than a close imitation of any one, although the influence of Alonso [de la Vega] seems to be the most immediate" (Eoff, pp. 86–87).

Arróniz, who offers a detailed summary of the Bandello tale, seems to agree with the thesis of Menéndez y Pelayo and Menéndez Pidal. On the other hand, Valli rejects that thesis, finding that in this *patraña* Timoneda follows his usual practice of combining elements from several sources; in this case, according to Valli, the Valencian added to the basic plot derived from Bandello, II, 44, elements from "the first part of *novella* 22 of Sabadino degli Arienti (*Le porretane*, Bologna, 1843) and . . . [from *novella*] 24, first part, of the same Bandello."[68] Once again the Valencian has challenged the source-hunters!

On esthetic grounds, Menéndez y Pelayo objects to the fact that Timoneda "left almost without explanation [the Duquesa's] trip to Santiago" but sixteenth-century readers of chivalric novels would not have been at all surprised at the *curiosity* that was the lady's sole motivation in Timoneda's account. The great polygraph correctly labels as "impertinent" the long letter in which the vassals of the Duquesa write to her father, for the message repeats to a great extent incidents that have already been narrated.

Widely diffused and extensively studied, the basic theme of this tale is the falsely accused lady who is defended by a champion who first ascertains her innocence by disguising himself as a confessor. In his *Rosa gentil*, Timoneda includes a well-known Spanish variant of the theme: "Ballad of How Count Ramón de Barcelona Freed the Empress of Germany Who Was About to Be Burned at the Stake" (*Primavera*, no. 162).[69]

*Patraña* VIII

Regarded as the most licentious story of the collection, the eighth *patraña* was omitted for this reason from the edition of Madrid, 1759:

The handsome King of Poland, Acrio, wishes to meet Octavio, who is as handsome as he or perhaps more so, according to Redulfo, Acrio's courtier and Octavio's brother. Redulfo persuades Octavio to visit Acrio. On the very morning of Octavio's departure for Acrio's court, he discovers by accident that his new wife Brasilda is unfaithful to him with a servant, the lowliest and most ignorant in the household. Shocked and torn between love for Brasilda and desire for vengeance, he goes on his way, giving the guilty pair no sign of his awareness. At Acrio's court, Octavio must remain in seclusion because his grief over Brasilda's infidelity causes him to lose his good looks. One day he discovers to his amazement that Acrio's queen, Olimpa, is committing adultery with an ugly dwarf. This new knowledge consoles him to the extent that he recovers his handsomeness. Exacting from him a promise not to harm the guilty pair, Octavio reveals to Acrio the infidelity of Olimpa, after having related Brasilda's. They agree to travel widely and discover whether the defect is only in their wives or in the feminine sex. In the course of discovering that female imperfection is universal, they acquire a young mistress who has been deflowered by a youth named Siriaco. Acrio, Octavio, and the girl set out for the royal court. One night the girl, as she lies between Acrio and Octavio, succeeds in satisfying the desire of Siriaco, who has promised to marry her if she sleeps the night with him. Each of her "regulars" thinks the other has engaged the girl. When they are told next day that such was not the case, they good-humoredly allow Siriaco and the girl to marry. They then are determined to return to their respective wives, "dissembling like the long-suffering and patient, for of such was the kingdom of God and they lived for many years on earth."

There is no doubt that Timoneda based his version of this cynical tale on the episode of Giocondo and Fiammetta in Canto 28 of the *Orlando furioso* by Lodovico Ariosto (1474–1533).[70] It is interesting to note that the Valencian author made indefinite the locale of the inn episode which, in Ariosto, occurs in the kingdom of Valencia.

Oriental in origin, this theme appears in the first story of *The Thousand and One Nights*. Salacious or not, the story of the two cuckolds is funny because of the very exaggeration required to prove the antifeminine thesis embodied in this *patraña*.

*Patraña* IX

Also indirectly related to the great collection of Arabic stories mentioned above, is the ninth tale:

Ceberino, son of the rich Barcelonese merchant Hilario, misspends a large sum of his father's money in Naples. On the night of his return to Barcelona penniless, Rosina mistakes him for the man with whom she plans to elope. Receiving some precious jewels from her, Ceberino pretends to be the desired man and they depart for Valencia. When Rosina discovers her error, Ceberino identifies himself, and in a wood they exchange vows and consummate their "marriage." At the nearby seashore Ceberino is captured by Turkish corsairs and carried off to Constantinople where the Grand Turk's daughter, Madama, falls in love with him under the name Rosino. Having seen her "husband" carried off, Rosina dresses in men's clothing, changes her name to Ceberino, and takes up residence in

Valencia. Madama gives Ceberino a small box of jewels, which he sends with some sailors to Spain for his parents. The jewel box ends up in Rosina's possession. Recognizing among the jewels the ring she gave Ceberino in the wood, Rosina is deeply troubled about her beloved's fate. Ceberino escapes on a Spanish ship that lands in Valencia, where he is reunited with Rosina. They travel to Barcelona and are formally joined in marriage.

Although realistic in background, this rapid-moving *patraña* suffers from being little more than an improbable series of coincidences. Even so, it has been intensively studied by investigators. Writing in about 1907, Menéndez y Pelayo thought that this was the only one of the *patrañas* that might be original with Timoneda (Menéndez y Pelayo, p. 77). Eoff points to certain resemblances between this narrative and one by Girolamo Parabosco—*I diporti*, II, 11—adding, however, that Parabosco's *novella* "is not close enough to Timoneda to be taken as the latter's source, but it serves to show that such stories as the one of Timoneda were being written, and makes it seem plausible that Timoneda was making use of some particular story, likely Italian" (Eoff, p. 90). He concludes by stating that "Timoneda often made additions and alterations of his own to stories that he followed in the main. It may be that such is the case with this *patraña*" (Eoff, p. 90). In 1946, Giorgio Valli, independently of Eoff's study, arrived at a similar conclusion. According to the Italian Hispanist, Timoneda constructed his *patraña* by adding to Parabosco's basic plot, cited above, elements from Sabadino degli Arienti's *Le porretane (novella* 22) and from diverse other sources. The *patraña* illustrates what he calls Timoneda's "system of incrustation" or mosaiclike method of combining elements. In 1955, another Italian scholar, Enrico Cerulli, without reference to Valli's study, undertook to delineate the sources of this narrative.

According to Cerulli, this ninth *patraña* is based on the story of Orio Doria and Policasta in the fortieth canto of the *Mambriano* by the fifteenth-century Italian Cieco da Ferrara. Timoneda may also have derived certain details of his story from another Italian work of the fifteenth century, the anonymous "Ottinello e Giulia." In turn, both these Italian accounts derive from an episode involving the prince Qamar al-zamān and the princess Budūr in the Arabic collection known as *The Thousand and One Nights*. Also derived from the Qamar al-zamān episode is an important analogue of the Italian and Spanish versions: the fifteenth-century French poem known as

*Pierre de Provence et la Belle Maghelonne.* Cerulli rejects the possibility of the latter's influence on Timoneda, but it should be noted that a version of the "Magalona" story is listed in the Inventory of the Valencian's books—a fact of which Cerulli was apparently unaware.

Two facts emerge from such discrepant views, as they will repeatedly: (1) Timoneda was an eclectic user of sources, and (2) his themes, though not original, were widely popular.

According to Asensio, this *patraña* "supplied the final scenes of the coarse *Entremés sin título,*" no. 21 in Cotarelo's famous *Colección de entremeses.*[71]

*Patraña* X

In his tenth *patraña*, Timoneda returns to the theme of cuckoldry:

Marquina, a barber's wife, is angry with her husband because he refuses to give her thirty ducats to buy a gold chain. Tancredo, a gentleman who wishes to seduce Marquina's next-door neighbor, a married woman named Celicea, promises Marquina the money if the latter helps him obtain the favors of Celicea. Marquina agrees and an assignation is arranged. However, that night Celicea's suspicious husband ties her to a pillar in the patio. Marquina, anxious for the promised money, takes Celicea's place at the pillar, sending the latter off to meet Tancredo. When the tied-up Marquina, supposedly his wife, doesn't answer him, Celicea's husband in anger cuts off her nose in the darkness. Celicea returns after her tryst and frees the noseless Marquina, who ties Celicea to the post and then collects the thirty ducats from Tancredo. Celicea now cries out for God to prove her innocent of her husband's suspicions by miraculously "restoring" her nose. When her husband sees her nose, he is convinced of her innocence. Meanwhile Marquina's husband, angry at her inadequate reply to a question, throws a knife case at her. She cries out that he has thereby cut off her nose. A passing *alcalde* arrests the barber, who is eventually sentenced to being flogged through the streets of the city. "Thus, because of a desire for a gold chain, the barber's wife lost her nose and her husband was flogged."

This comic, unexemplary story is very ancient, its origins having been traced by Eoff as far back as the *Panchatantra*, a collection of tales of the third or fourth century A.D., written in Sanskrit (Eoff, pp. 90–96). From Sanskrit the tale was translated into Pahlavic

(Middle Persian) and thence into Arabic, in the eighth-century *Kalilah and Dimnah* (or *Fables of Bidpai* or *Pilpay.*)

The story then entered Europe through this Arabic collection which appeared in a number of translations, the most important of which are: (1) *Calila e Dymna*, an Old Spanish translation made in the thirteenth century, (2) a Latin version by John of Capua, *Directorium Humanae Vitae*, printed about 1480, and (3) a Spanish version of Capua, *Ejemplario contra los engaños y peligros del mundo*, first printed at Zaragoza in 1493. Eoff concludes that the above-mentioned *Directorium* "seems to be the most logical choice, perhaps, of any of the translations, for the source of Timoneda."

Among the many analogues of this tale, two of the most notable are Boccaccio, *Decameron*, VII, 8, and *Les Cent Nouvelles Nouvelles*, no. 38 (first edition, 1486). Both of them differ in significant details from the *patraña;* for example, in the French version, the wife's lover is a Franciscan friar.

The fact that Marquina is responsible for her husband's being arrested and punished recalls the vindictive wives of *patraña* III and the *Sobremesa*, I, 20. H. Recoules sees in this *patraña* the source of the anonymous seventeenth-century *entremés* entitled *El cuero.*[72]

*Patraña* XI

The short, earthy *patraña* X is followed by the longest story in the collection, *patraña* XI:

King Antioco of Antioch is carrying on an incestuous relationship with his daughter Safirea. In order to fend off her suitors, he promises her hand to the man who solves a certain riddle, with the warning that, in case of failure, the suitor will be decapitated. Prince Apolonio of Tyre solves the riddle—which involves an allusion to the royal incest—but the King refuses to allow the marriage. Disconsolate, Apolonio returns to Tyre and from there goes to Tarcia (Tarsus), where he saves the population from starvation. Later, he marries Silvania, the daughter of the King of Pentopolitania (Pentapolis). It is agreed that Apolonio will succeed to the throne on his father-in-law's demise. When the Prince sets out to take possession of Antioch, which Safirea has bequeathed to him, and to recover Tyre from an invading enemy, a storm hits his fleet, his pregnant wife gives birth prematurely to a daughter, and Silvania appears to die. Unbeknown to Apolonio, however, she is restored to health in Ephesus. The Prince leaves his daughter Politania in Tarcia while he goes on to Antioch. After a number of vicissitudes, the girl is taken by corsairs to Ephesus, where she is sold to Lenio, master of a brothel. She persuades Lenio to allow her to pay him by making her living as a singer and musician. She becomes known as "la Truhanilla" ("The Entertainer").

After fourteen or fifteen years, during which he has recaptured Tyre, Apolonio returns to Antioch and then to Tarcia. Here he is told that Politania is dead. On the way to Pentopolitania a storm forces the grief-stricken Apolonio to land in Ephesus, where he is well received by Prince Palimedo. As part of the entertainment, "la Truhanilla" sings for Apolonio, including a ballad about her life, which causes him to recognize that she is his daughter. A great celebration follows, resulting in Silvania's learning that her husband and daughter are in Ephesus. The reunion of the three takes place. Palimedo asks for and obtains Politania's hand in marriage, receiving as dowry the principality of Tyre and the kingdom of Antioch. After the wedding celebration, Apolonio and Silvania depart for Pentopolitania. The joy of seeing them again after twenty years brings on the death of Silvania's father, leaving Apolonio the sole king of all Pentopolitania. "And we are left rather pleased at what we have heard in his pleasant story."

After reviewing the pertinent bibliography, Homero Serís argues persuasively that, for his version of the story of Apollonius of Tyre, Timoneda used the recently rediscovered *Novela de Apolonio*, [Zaragoza?: Pablo Hurus de Constancia?, c. 1488?].[73] This work in Castilian prose is, in the main, a translation of the famous *Gesta Romanorum*, Ch. 153. The Valencian follows his model closely, but, as usual, introduces certain interesting alterations, along with some name changes—for example, Tarsia, the name of Apollonius' daughter in the original, becomes Politania. Like the former, Politania is a musician-singer but she is a more Spanish one dressed in her *sayuelo* (blouse) and *zaragüelles* (breeches), and playing the *guitarrilla* (small guitar) and *sonajas* (tambourine). Timoneda, while eliminating Tarsia's adeptness at riddles, enhances Politania's musicianship by including two of her songs: a *canción* (twelve lines) and a *romance* (sixty-six lines), which are presumably of his own invention. Two verses of the former ("see how at times sorrow / turns into much greater joy") are an allusion, as Serís notes, to the *Incipit* of the *Novela de Apolonio*, which reads: "Here begins the life and history of King Apolonio, which shows how temporary tribulation changes in the end to lasting joy." Timoneda omits Tarsia's only song, an archaic twelve-line stanza of Alexandrine verses. The Valencian also modified his source by adding an exchange of songs between Silvania (a sonnet) and Apolonio (an octave) on the occasion of their first meeting.

The significance of the Apollonius theme in European literature has been panoramically described by A. H. Smyth:

> The Apollonius Saga . . . is known to nearly every language of Europe, and persists through more than a thousand years, flourishing in extraordinary popularity. . . . From its untraced origin in the late sophistic romance of Greece it entered the literatures of Europe through a hundred manuscripts of an early Latin version. It was popular in Italy, Russia, Hungary, Bohemia, Norway and Iceland; it is found in a Danish ballad and a Netherland drama; it was sung by Provençal poets, and beyond the Pyrenees; . . . it was translated in Crete into modern Greek in the sixteenth century; it was absorbed in France into the cycle of Charlemagne, and it is the only romance in Anglo-Saxon literature. The mythical Apollonius tossing on strange seas about the Mediterranean coasts became a veritable hero of history to the Germans, French and Italians, in the eleventh, twelfth and thirteenth centuries.
>
> The long line of translations, imitations, *märchen*, *volksbücher*, *sagas*, romances, ballads and plays, ends at last in the culminating splendor of Shakespeare's *Pericles Prince of Tyre*.[74]

Finally, mention must be made of the fact that some critics have seen in the chaste figure of the entertainer Tarsia /Politania an antecedent of Cervantes' Preciosa *(La Gitanilla)* and of Victor Hugo's Esmeralda *(Notre Dame de Paris)*.

To retell this Byzantine or Milesian tale from memory would have been difficult indeed. In outline, the peregrinations of Apolonio alone look like this: Tyre → Antioch → Tyre → Tarcia → Pentopolitania → Tarcia → Antioch → Tyre → Antioch → Tarcia → Ephesus → Pentopolitania.

*Patraña* XII

After the involved and exemplary story of Apollonius, Timoneda places one of his shortest *patrañas*, the twelfth, which was intended to be comic:

An avaricious blind man has the habit of counting his money each evening after clearing his hut of any possible intruders by means of knife thrusts. A neighbor discovers the existence of the money and steals it one morning during the blind man's absence. The next day the thief follows the blind man, who tells his trouble to another blind man. The latter says no one could get his money because he carries it in the lining of his cap, at which point the thief seizes the cap and flees. The second blind man accuses the first of stealing the cap, an argument ensues and, as the thief escapes with the two blind men's money, they beat each other with sticks.

Like the first, seventh, and other *patrañas,* this one illustrates the overlapping or interrelationship between theater and prose fiction; it is a variant of the playlet entitled *Paso de dos ciegos y un mozo muy gracioso para la noche de Navidad* published by Timoneda in the *Turiana* (1565). In the play, the thief is not the first blind man's neighbor but rather his young guide. In both the play and the *patraña,* the author insists on the miserliness of the first blind man; the second blind man, in both cases, is boastful of his ability to outwit possible thieves. Precisely these characteristics of the two blind men make somewhat more comprehensible our ancestors' ability to laugh at such unfortunates. But more on this subject in our discussion of the play.

Eoff cites a number of Italian facetiae that resemble the basic motif of the *patraña,* the most similar being one by Lodovico Domenichi in which "two blind men one morning are discussing their earnings and one of them reveals that he carries his money in his cap. A poor man nearby overhears and grabs the cap. The blind man, thinking that the other blind man has stolen his cap, quarrels with him and a fight ensues" (Eoff, pp. 121–22). Readers of Spanish literature may be reminded of the blind man and Lazarillo de Tormes in the famous novel of this title.

H. Recoules has proved conclusively that this *patraña* is the source of two seventeenth-century *entremeses: El gato y la montera* by Manuel de León Marchante and *Los ciegos* by Antonio García del Portillo and Maestro Albolafio.[75] More difficult to prove, however, is Recoules' opinion that the *patraña* antedated and inspired Timoneda's *entremés* on this theme.

### *Patraña* XIII

From the brutal realism of the preceding story, Timoneda turns to a farfetched tale of sorcery in *patraña* XIII:

The rich Feliciano's daughter is kidnapped and abandoned by his brother so that she cannot inherit her father's wealth. The child is found by a wealthy farmer named Erasistrato and is reared by his wife, who calls her Zarcina (after the brambles [zarzas] among which she was found). Roselia, Feliciano's wife, dies in giving birth to a son, named Roselio after her. From rage Feliciano's brother dies shortly thereafter. One day while hunting, Feliciano saves from a lioness Erasistrato's blood daughter whom he names Leonarda. Roselio falls in love with Zarcina; not knowing that they are brother and sister, they promise to marry each other, but Roselio is obliged by his father to marry Leonarda. Erasistrato sues for breach of promise. Feliciano sends Roselio to Macedonia, where he becomes a friend of Corineo, who is having an affair with a married woman named Crisolora. Roselio returns home. A relative of Crisolora discovers her affair with Corineo and challenges the latter to a duel. On the advice of a sorcerer friend, Corineo asks Roselio to substitute for him. Roselio agrees.

Before the latter's departure for Macedonia, the sorcerer causes an exchange of appearance in Roselio and Corineo. Roselio gets Corineo to promise to marry Zarcina, if need be, and then departs with the sorcerer for Macedonia. Corineo—as Roselio—refrains from sexual relations with Roselio's wife, Leonarda. When so ordered by the court, he agrees to marry Zarcina. Leonarda learns of this marriage; Roselio returns from Macedonia after defeating Corineo's opponent. Both Roselio and Corineo have been restored to their own appearance by the sorcerer. Roselio explains to Feliciano and Leonarda what has been going on. Erasistrato is satisfied that Zarcina is married to Corineo. It is discovered that she is actually Feliciano's lost daughter. Soon too it is learned that Leonarda is Erasistrato's daughter and that Corineo is his son. (Concerning the latter anagnorisis [recognition scene], Timoneda mercifully spares the reader all details, stating merely that "at this point it came to be discovered that Corineo was Erasistrato's son, whom he hadn't seen for ten years"). So to the delight of all it turns out that brother and sister, Roselio and Zarcina, are married to brother and sister, Leonarda and Corineo.

At the conclusion of this absurd tale, Timoneda states, "Of the preceding story there exists a play called *La Feliciana.*" Once again, we see the interrelationship of theater and prose fiction as well as the practice of deriving a play's name by adjectivizing a character's name: Feliciano > Feliciana > *Comedia Feliciana.* Unfortunately (or perhaps fortunately) the play in question is not extant, nor is anything else known about it. It may safely be assumed to have been the source of this *patraña;*[76] cf. *patrañas* I, VII, and XV.

Once more, also, sorcery plays an important role in this story as it did in *patraña* IV; see too the sorcerers of the plays *Carmelia, Paliana, Aurelia,* and *Floriana.*

*Patraña* XIV

After the preceding story of literary origin, Timoneda refreshingly turns again to the folktale in his *patraña* XIV:

In order for him to keep his abbotship, a king requires an abbot to answer the following questions within a month:

1. "What am I worth?"
2. "Where is the center of the earth?"
3. "What am I thinking?"

Learning of the abbot's problem, the monastery cook offers to take his place before the king and answer the questions.

The cook's answers are:

1. "You are worth twenty-nine pieces of silver since Christ was worth thirty."
2. "The center of the earth is where your Highness puts his feet. This is because, since the world is round like a ball, wherever the foot is placed is the middle of it."
3. "You are thinking you are talking with the abbot but are actually talking to his cook."

The king confirms the abbot for life and grants many benefits to the cook.

This version of the tale known to folklorists as "The King and the Abbot" is derived from Spanish oral tradition, according to Menéndez y Pelayo (III, 88–90), Eoff (pp. 125–31), and Espinosa,[77] rather than from a literary source, as suggested by Schevill.[78] Espinosa demonstrates the amazing vitality of this theme by adding a dozen additional Hispanic versions to those noted by Walter Anderson in his classic study of some 561 European and Asian versions of the tale. More recently Professor Ben-Amos has studied an Americanized Jewish oral version, which is interesting in the light of Anderson's belief that the oldest known version, by a ninth-century Arabic historian, is based on earlier Jewish sources.[79] "The King and the Abbot" has survived, too, among the Spanish-speaking inhabitants of Colorado and New Mexico, as reported by J. B. Rael.[80]

In the notes to his edition of the *Patrañuelo* (Madrid: Castilla, 1948, pp. 228–235), Alberto Sánchez quotes the full text of a modern literary version of this story, "La gramática parda" by Antonio de Trueba (1819–1889), thus providing the reader with an excellent chance to compare Timoneda's spare, rapid-paced narration with a longer, more artistic version. The comparison demonstrates how Timoneda's *patrañas,* in their refreshing brevity, are often really outlines of stories.

*Patraña* XV

Also surviving in the American Southwest are versions of the story told in Timoneda's *patraña* XV:

Casiodoro goes on a business trip to Ferrara, leaving his wife, Finea, in Candia. Falacio bets Casiodoro one hundred ducats that Finea would be unfaithful to him if given the chance. Falacio goes to Candia and is unsuccessful in his attempt to seduce Finea but, with the aid of old Crispina, he obtains several hairs from a mole on Finea's back as well as the exact description of her room and bed. On this basis Falacio convinces Casiodoro that the latter has lost the bet. The unhappy Casiodoro returns to Candia. Because he still loves Finea, he has decided to abandon her on a desert island instead of killing her. Thus abandoned, Finea dresses as a man and assumes the name Pedro in order to better protect her chastity. "Pedro" is picked up by a passing vessel and is taken to Cyprus where "he" becomes royal secretary and chief accountant of the kingdom. Casiodoro and his father-in-law, Herodiano, become involved in a lawsuit over the former's treatment of the latter, who also demands an account of his daughter. "Pedro" passes from the service of the King of Cyprus to that of the King of "his" native Candia, who soon makes "him" his Chief Justice. In this capacity "he" is called upon to settle the suit between Casiodoro and Herodiano. In this way the truth is discovered. Falacio and Crispina are punished and Finea lived with her husband "many happy and prosperous years in the city of Candia."

The *patraña* ends with the words: "Of the preceding tale there exists a play entitled *Eufemia.*" Timoneda probably refers here to Lope de Rueda's play of this title, which the Valencian author published in the same year, 1567, that saw the appearance of the *Patrañuelo.* In turn, Rueda's *Eufemia,* like Shakespeare's *Cymbeline,* is usually thought to have been derived from Boccaccio, *Decameron,*

II, 9.[81] The four works in question are certainly analogues, but their many significant differences point to several possibilities: the influence of individual inventiveness, the use of additional sources, or the introduction of folk elements. The latter possibility is strongly suggested by the existence of four Southwestern Spanish folktales that have many elements in common with this *patraña* (Rael, vol. I, no. 130, no. [131], no. 132, no. 138).

Elise Richter[82] sees the possible influence of this *patraña* on Shakespeare's *Cymbeline*, but there is no solid evidence that the *Patrañuelo* was known in early seventeenth-century England.

E. B. Place believes that María de Zayas y Sotomayor (1590–1661?) was indebted to the figure of Finea in the guise of a judge for a similar episode in her *El juez de su causa.*[83]

*Patraña* XVI

For this *patraña*, Timoneda turns to a story about a hero of antiquity, Cyrus the Great, c. 600–529 B.C., King of Persia:

Astiages, King of Media, has on several occasions a dream which is interpreted by his sages to mean that his daughter Mandane will give birth to a son who will deprive him of the kingdom. When Mandane gives birth to a son, Astiages orders his servant Harpago to kill the child but the servant delivers him to a shepherd who, instead of abandoning the infant as ordered, rears him as his own at the request of his wife, who has just lost a child. When the boy, named Ciro (Cyrus) after the shepherd's wife Cira, is ten years old his true identity becomes known to Astiages as a result of a game in which a group of boys choose Cyrus to be their king. Thinking that the latter kingship constitutes fulfillment of his dream, Astiages abandons his fear of Cyrus but punishes the disobedient Harpago by serving him a meal in which the latter's only son has been cooked. Years later, Harpago, desirous of vengeance, writes to Cyrus, who is now a famous soldier in Persia, telling him that he will help him gain the throne of Media from Astiages. With Harpago's aid, Cyrus does defeat Astiages, whom he then imprisons in a castle. He greatly honors Harpago. "And from then on the monarchy of the Medes died and Cyrus passed it to the Persians."

Manuel F. Galiano has shown convincingly that Timoneda based this *patraña* on a ballad, "En la provincia de Media," published by Lorenzo de Sepúlveda in Antwerp in 1551 (reprinted in Durán, *Romancero general*, I, no. 492).[84] This same conclusion was reached independently by Rafael Ferreres (p. 171). Sepúlveda's ballad, in turn, derives from Justin's epitome of Pompeius Trogus' condensation of the Greek historian Herodotus. Justin's Latin work appeared in a Spanish translation by Jorge de Bustamente in Alcalá, 1540.

The ghastly episode in which Harpago unwittingly consumes his son's cooked body recalls Timoneda's ballad "Filomena entre pastores" (*Rosa de amores*, fol. 60) and his play *Filomena*, in both of which King Tereus unknowingly consumes the cooked body of his son Itys.

The Cyrus legend also inspired Lope de Vega's play *Contra valor no hay desdicha*, which seems to have been based mainly on Justin's epitome.

*Patraña* XVII

The tables are delightfully but fatally turned on a slanderer in *patraña* XVII:

The King of Thrace takes into his service a youth of fifteen named Julián, the son of humble parents. When the King appoints Julián as his gentleman cupbearer to replace Estacio, the latter is angry and tells the youth in secret to turn his head away when he speaks to the King because he offends the King with his bad breath. Estacio then tells the King that Julián turns his head away because, according to Julián, the King has bad breath. The King decides to have Julián killed. He orders some charcoal burners to throw into their fire a servant whom he will send the following day and who will ask: "Have you done what the King ordered you?" The next day the King sends Julián to the charcoal burners' kiln, telling him to ask them if they have carried out his orders.

But on the way the youth stops in a church to say some prayers. Estacio, knowing of the King's plan and anxious to see it effected, goes to the charcoal burners and asks if they have done what the King ordered. He is immediately cast into the fire. When Julián arrives and asks the same question, he is told that they have carried out the King's orders. As Estacio does not return, the King questions Julián and discovers the plot of the envious Estacio. He concludes that justice has been done and henceforth loves Julián much more.

Menéndez y Pelayo (III, 87–88) and Eoff (pp. 138–40) trace the origins of this famous tale to an ancient Sanskrit story by Somadeva, believing that Timoneda's immediate source was probably the *Gesta*

*Romanorum.*[85] On the other hand, Enrico Cerulli, in an extensive and erudite study, arrives at a different conclusion.[86]

According to the Italian scholar, this *patraña*—which combines the two motifs that he calls "the King's mouth" and "the slanderer cast into the furnace"—is probably based on some Italian *Book of the Miracles of Mary* (see the manuscript version he transcribes on p. 111). Among the numerous analogues he cites are versions in Medieval Latin, French, Italian, Catalan, Hebrew, Arabic, Ethiopic (Geez), Turkish, and Amharic. The oldest Western version known today is that of the Englishman Walter Map (Mapes) in his *De Nugis Curialium* (1191–1193), while the oldest Oriental redaction cited by Cerulli is found in the Arabic *Sukkardān* (1356) of Ibn Abi Ḥağala.

It is interesting to note how the story has been adapted to different cultures. In some versions, the use of garlic becomes part of the bad-breath motif; in others, leprosy is allegedly involved. In some versions the intended victim is saved on account of his devotion to the Virgin Mary or to the Mass, or to both; in others, he is saved because he stops in a synagogue.

Cerulli also assembles from many languages, including Greek and Russian, a very large number of partial analogues of this *patraña.* For example, the forty-eighth poem of Alphonse the Wise's *Cantigas de Santa María* combines the motif of slander (here indeterminate) with that of "the slanderer cast into the furnace." The intended victim is saved when he stops at a church to hear a Mass of the Virgin Mary. In the fifteenth-century *Libro de los exemplos por a.b.c.* by Clemente Sánchez de Vercial, story no. 8 joins the "false accusation of adultery" motif with the "slanderer cast into the furnace" motif. Again it is the Marian devotion of the intended victim that saves his life. Another Iberian variant is the legend known as "the page of St. Elizabeth of Portugal" in which the motif of slander (false accusation of adultery) is combined with that of "the slanderer cast into the furnace." The page is saved because he stops to hear Mass.

An interesting variation on the last legend is found in the play *Santa Isabel, reina de Portugal* by Francisco de Rojas Zorrilla (1607–1648).

### *Patraña* XVIII

In *patraña* XVIII, one friend teaches another a practical lesson "the hard way":

Each day, the tailor Claudino greets his friend the hosier Filemo with the same wish: "May God guard you from an evil man [or] an evil woman." One day Filemo, annoyed, tells him not to say that anymore. A few days later Claudino borrows two ducats from Filemo, giving him valuable collateral. Claudino returns the money the same day. Two weeks later the tailor borrows five ducats from the hosier without collateral and returns them three days later. Not long after that, Claudino borrows ten ducats. He doesn't return them, however, so that eventually Filemo is obliged to require him to appear before a judge. To do so, Claudino says, he must borrow a cape from Filemo. Wearing the borrowed cape, Claudino tells the judge that he has returned the money, adding that Filemo is even capable of claiming to own the cape he (Claudino) is wearing. Filemo of course does claim to be the cape's owner. The judge tells Claudino to swear whether or not he owes the ten ducats. When Claudino swears ambiguously that his cape is as much Filemo's as it is true that he owes him the money, the judge, misunderstanding the ambiguity, frees Claudino. That night Claudino returns to the hosier his cape and the ten ducats, explaining that he has done all this to show what an evil man or an evil woman can do. "Then Filemo embraced him, thanking him from then on for the advice that he gave him."

Menéndez y Pelayo (p. 82n) sees the source of this *patraña* in Sabadino degli Arienti's *novella* 20 of *Le porretane* (1510). A detailed comparison of the *patraña* and the *novella* leads Eoff (pp. 141–43) to the conclusion that the many notable differences suggest either an intermediate version, or the oral transmission of the Italian's story, or simply alterations introduced by the Valencian on his own.[87]

### *Patraña* XIX

In his *patraña* XIX, Timoneda returns to a familiar chivalric theme, the princess who is falsely accused of illicit sexual activity:

Aquileyo, King of Scotland, in gratitude for divine assistance, becomes a monk at the Abbey of Santa Flor. He is succeeded on the throne by his brother Calimedes, whose beautiful daughter Brandiana immediately attracts such suitors as Ricardo and Dulcido, the sons of the King of Brittany, and Tancredo, son of the Duke of Albania. Ricardo is favored from the first. Promising her a dowry of seven thousand ducats if she succeeds, Tancredo has Febea, his mistress and a friend of Brandiana, intercede for him with the Princess. But to no avail. Next, Tancredo tells Ricardo the lie that he has been sleeping every night with Brandiana and that his rival may witness their lovemaking. Tancredo arranges with Febea that at their next tryst she dress like and imitate Brandiana so that he can rid himself, he says, of his obsession with the latter. Having seen and heard Tancredo with the supposed Brandiana, Ricardo is about to commit suicide but is saved by his brother Dulcido.

Ricardo, next day, after telling a shepherd to report his suicide to be the result of Brandiana's infidelity, jumps into the sea, but, changing his mind, swims to the Abbey of Santa Flor, where he is given refuge. The shepherd delivers the message. Dulcido before the royal court asserts Brandiana's guilt and declares himself ready to defend his assertion in combat. Calimedes promises his daughter in marriage to the man who defeats Dulcido. Informed of the King's promise, Ricardo, his identity hidden, decides after much wrestling with his conscience to engage his brother in combat in defense of Brandiana's honor. Nightfall interrupts the combat. Meanwhile Febea, realizing her complicity in Tancredo's plot and desirous of preventing the death of the combatants, confesses all to the monk Aquileyo, who informs his brother Calimedes of Brandiana's innocence. Tancredo and Febea are arrested but are freed later, at Ricardo's request. The latter will receive Brandiana's hand in marriage.

According to Menéndez y Pelayo (p. 83), the common source of this *patraña* as well as a *novella* of Giraldi (*Ecatommiti*, Introduction, 9) and Shakespeare's *Much Ado About Nothing* is to be found in Matteo Bandello, Part I, no. 22. The latter *novella*, he believes, derives in part from the episode of Ginevra and Rinaldo in Canto V of Ariosto's *Orlando furioso*, an episode that is indebted to a similar one in the great Catalan novel *Tirant lo Blanc*. Eoff, however, shows by means of detailed comparison that Timoneda, though introducing changes, is much closer to Ariosto than to Bandello (Eoff, pp. 143–47). This opinion is shared by Rafael Ferreres (p. 185).

The present tale repeats certain motifs that have been seen in *patraña* VII: the false accusation of sexual misconduct, the defense of the lady by her incognito beloved, and the role of auricular confession. In VII, the Duchess reveals her innocence to the Count disguised as a priest who has come to hear her confession; in XIX, Febea reveals the Princess's innocence in her confession to the monk Aquileyo, Brandiana's uncle.

In this *patraña* there occurs one of the rare passages in which Timoneda slows down his rapid action-packed narration long enough to give the reader a glimpse of the inner life of one of his characters. Following his decision to defend Brandiana's honor in combat with his brother, Ricardo takes leave of the monks, after asking for their prayers, and sets out for the royal court. At this point, Timoneda comments: ". . . not to be forgotten is the fact that along the way he was wavering within himself and stopping from time to time to say"—here the author quotes at some length Ricardo's thoughts as he ponders the dilemma of engaging in mortal combat with his own brother for the sake of his beloved Brandiana.

*Patraña* XX

In his *patraña* XX, Timoneda uses the same motif of the false accusation of sexual misconduct but set in very different circumstances:

In Naples, Firmiano, the widowed father of Machabelo, marries Cavina, with whom he has another son, Modesto. Cavina falls in love with her young stepson and openly declares to him her desire. Shocked, the boy puts her off by telling her to wait until his father goes to their country estate. When Firmiano leaves, Machabelo again puts off his stepmother, whose love then turns to profound hatred. With the aid of the slave Ganejo she obtains poison with which to kill the youth, but her son Modesto drinks the substance and collapses. She tells Firmiano that Machabelo is responsible for the death and that he tried to rape her. At the judicial trial that ensues, Ganejo testifies against Machabelo, who, defending himself, reveals his stepmother's advances. One of the judges, who is a lawyer and physician, reveals that he had sold the alleged poison to the slave for five ducats but, being suspicious of him, he did so on the condition that the coins be kept in a small sack, sealed with the slave's ring, until they could be properly weighed. The small sack is produced, the seal is matched with the ring, and tortures are applied, but the slave does not confess. The doctor then declares that, in view of his suspicions, he did not give Ganejo a true poison but rather a sleeping potion. Soon Modesto appears, thus confirming the doctor's story as well as Machabelo's innocence. Machabelo is freed. The slave confesses and is sentenced to be hanged. Cavina is banished from the kingdom and the doctor is granted the five ducats. Firmiano returns home with his two sons.

In a detailed comparison Eoff proves conclusively that Timoneda's *patraña* XX follows very closely its Italian model: Ser Giovanni, *Il pecorone*, XXIII, 2 (Eoff, pp. 147–51). In places the Valencian does little more than translate the Italian original. He does, however, give names to the characters, whereas Ser Giovanni does not.

Tracing the origins of this folk theme, Eoff notes that "the subject matter of this *patraña* is older in a written form than that of any of the other *patrañas*. The first written story containing this theme is the Egyptian tale of the *Two Brothers*, which . . . was written about the 14th century B.C." (Eoff, pp. 147–48). Other analogues mentioned by the American scholar are: the story of Phaedra and Hippolytus in Greek mythology; the story of Joseph and Potiphar's wife in the Old Testament; Lucius Apuleius, *The Golden Ass*, Ch. 44, etc.

*Patraña* XXI

In *patraña* XXI, Timoneda once again uses the theme of false accusation of sexual misconduct, which here sets in motion a very complicated plot:

Before setting out on a pilgrimage to Jerusalem, Marcelo, King of England, orders that all obey his pious wife, Geroncia, whom he commends to the care of his brother Pompeo. The latter soon tries to woo his sister-in-law, producing false letters saying that the King has died. Geroncia has Pompeo locked up. After a year and a half, when she receives word that the King is about to return, she tells the imprisoned Pompeo that she will free him on the condition that they both keep quiet about what has happened. The treacherous Pompeo appears in a shabby state before his brother who, when he asks for an explanation, is told by Pompeo that Geroncia had him imprisoned for refusing to commit adultery. In a rage, Marcelo orders two lackeys, Robledo and Lobatón, to take Geroncia to Brambly Woods and there to kill her. When Lobatón attempts to rape her beforehand, a scuffle ensues in which Robledo is killed. Lobatón again attempts to rape her but is killed by the Marquis of Delia, who happens upon the scene. Geroncia identifies herself to him as the maid Clariquea and expresses a desire to serve him. He takes her to France, where she becomes nursemaid to his two-year-old son. Fabricio, the brother of the Marquis, desires Clariquea but is rejected. As revenge, he kills his nephew with a knife and blames her for it. She is taken to Unfortunate Island and abandoned there. The knife which killed the child is hung over the city gate.

On the island, Geroncia/Clariquea finds a curative herb and not long after, she is rescued. Taken to the marquesate of Delia, she now calls herself Pelegrina (Pilgrim) and works for more than two years in a hospital, effecting cures with the mysterious herb and through her prayers. Fabricio is severely wounded one day when the hanging knife falls in a wind. Pelegrina promises to cure him provided that he confesses his sins and receives Communion first; and provided that he seeks the pardon of any person whom he has gravely injured. Accordingly, Fabricio confesses his guilt to the Marquis and his wife; they forgive him. Pelegrina then effects a cure. As a reward she is taken to London according to her request. Marcelo has not remarried. Pompeo is wounded in a tourney. Pelegrina advises that if he is to be cured he must meet the same conditions that have been stated above in the case of Fabricio. Pompeo confesses his guilt to Marcelo and is forgiven. Pelegrina then cures him. As her reward Pelegrina asks the King to marry her. She then reveals that she is Geroncia and asks that the two end their lives in God's service, leaving the kingdom in the hands of Pompeo. Shortly thereafter Marcelo and Geroncia entered monasteries "where they ended their days in great holiness."

Investigators do not agree concerning the exact source or sources of this *patraña*. As the ultimate source, Eoff argues persuasively in favor of Gautier de Coinci's verse *Miracles de Notre Dame* (1218–1222) which, in the fourteenth century, appeared in a Spanish prose translation. His detailed comparison of the two works shows that the action of the *patraña* and that of the prose translation are indeed "practically identical." His conclusion, then, is: "Since Timoneda's story is so nearly that of Gautier, it seems only reasonable to consider Gautier his source; in what particular copy or translation, however, whether the Old Spanish translation or some other copy now unknown, it would be difficult to say" (Eoff, p. 157).

The following works have been adduced by other scholars as possible sources or analogues, whether partial or otherwise: (1) *Florence de Rome,* a French narrative poem of the thirteenth century; (2) *Gesta Romanorum* (Ch. 249 in ed. Hermann Oesterley)[88] of the fourteenth century; (3) *Cuento muy fermoso del emperador Ottas et de la infanta Florencia su hija et del buen caballero Esmere,* a Spanish prose version of (1), dated as of the end of the fourteenth century or beginning of the fifteenth; (4) Ser Giovanni, *Il pecorone*, X, 1; and (5) Ariosto, *Orlando furioso*, XIII, 20–29.

According to E. B. Place, María de Zayas y Sotomayor (1590–1661?) "borrowed the substance of her story" *La perseguida triunfante* from this *patraña*.[89]

*Patraña* XXII

In the collection's last tale, *patraña* XXII, Timoneda makes use of look-alikes, as he did in his first *patraña*, and turns once more to Boccaccio for his inspiration:

The Roman proconsul Sergio sends his son Urbino to study at the University in Bologna, where the boy resides with Guillermo, a wealthy friend of Sergio. Urbino is reared with Guillermo's son Federico, the youths becoming very close friends. Urbino falls in love with Antonia, keeping the matter a secret from everyone including Federico. At this point marriage is arranged between Antonia and Federico. Urbino confesses to Federico his love for Antonia, and, being look-alikes, the two agree to exchange places on the following day when the betrothal is to take place. The ruse succeeds; with parental approval Urbino and Antonia sleep together, and the next day Urbino and Federico confess to Guillermo what they have done. Guillermo is angry but doesn't say so. He informs Antonia's parents, who are also angry but say nothing. Sergio arrives for the wedding and takes the couple back to Rome with him.

Not long after, Guillermo dies as a result of an illness brought on by his displeasure with what Federico did. His creditors, abetted by Antonia's still angry relatives, consume his estate so that Federico is left in poverty. He goes to Rome, where he begs in front of Urbino's home but is not recognized by the latter. In despair he goes to live and die in a cave outside the city. Two thieves come to the cave; in a dispute over distribution of stolen jewels, one kills the other and then flees with the loot. The police arrive and arrest Federico who, in his desire to die, confesses to having killed the dead thief. Urbino chances to be present at Federico's murder trial; he recognizes his friend and to save Federico declares himself guilty of the murder. Each friend claims to be the culprit. The real thief-murderer happens to witness this noble conduct and, conscience-stricken, confesses. The judge orders Urbino to take Federico home and sentences the murderer to life imprisonment instead of death. Urbino marries Federico to a sister of his and shares his wealth with him. "And they lived very happily and prosperously for many years as good and loyal friends."

It is generally agreed that the Valencian's *patraña* is a close adaptation of Boccaccio's *Decameron*, X, 8, and Eoff's detailed comparison proves it (pp. 157–60).

Of Oriental origin, the theme of the two friends entered Western Europe through the twelfth-century *Disciplina Clericalis* in which Pedro Alfonso (Moseh Sefardi), a converted Aragonese Jew, translated Arabic sources into Latin. From Pedro Alfonso the story passed into the *Gesta Romanorum* (Ch. 171) and the *Decameron*.

In his excellent study of Peninsular versions of this theme, Avalle-Arce describes a pertinent example of the theme's migratory behavior: Timoneda's version, derived largely from Boccaccio, inspired a version by Gonçalo Fernandes Trancoso (in his *Histórias de proveito e exemplo*, Lisbon, 1575?), which, in turn, influenced Matías de los Reyes' narrative *El curial del Parnaso* (Madrid, 1624).[90] "Thus we have an originally Spanish story (Pedro Alfonso) that directly or indirectly passed into Italian (Boccaccio), thence into Castilian (Timoneda) and from the latter into Portuguese (Trancoso) in order to return, finally, to Castilian (Reyes)."[91]

Timoneda brings his collection of adaptations to a close with two *quintillas* in which he asks the reader to forgive any faults he may find. In begging such indulgence, as he had also done at the end of the *Sobremesa*, he was following a practice that not only goes back to the playwrights of antiquity but would also be very popular among Spanish dramatists of the seventeenth century.

From specific cases cited in the preceding pages, it is clear that for his plots Timoneda borrowed freely and that he was also borrowed from. In these concluding paragraphs I shall discuss, in more general terms, the influence of Timoneda's prose fiction. At times, numerous anecdotes from the Valencian's collections were incorporated into other anthologies. A particularly interesting example is cited by Mérimée and Morley, who point out that "many of the tales in the *Alivio de caminantes* are to be found in the compilation called *La silva curiosa* (Paris, 1583) by the Navarrese Julián de Medrano. Remodeled in 1608 by the language teacher César Oudin, and enriched by the addition of Cervantes' *Curioso impertinente*, the *Silva* served as a Spanish text in France."[92] F. De Haan's collation of the *Biblioteca de autores españoles* edition of the *Sobremesa y alivio de caminantes* with Medrano's book shows that the latter took five of the stories attributed to Juan Aragonés and forty-two from the other two *partes.*[93]

Asensio[94] and Recoules have pointed out the popularity of the Valencian's prose fiction as a source for *entremesistas* (writers of *entremeses*). The first investigator, in addition to the example mentioned above on page 57, describes the transformation of *Buen aviso*, II, 87, in the *entremés Los habladores*, often attributed to Cervantes. Along with the cases cited above on pages 26, 58, 61, Recoules shows that *Sobremesa*, I, 22, inspired the anonymous seventeenth-century *entremés La muela.*

But it was not only the *entremesistas* who made use of Timoneda's prose fiction. In the words of M. A. Buchanan, "That collections of anecdotes like Timoneda's, Cruz's and others, were thoroughly ransacked by dramatists in search of material is an axiom."[95] Buchanan's data permit the following collations, each story of column A being found in the corresponding play of column B:

| *A* | *B* |
|---|---|
| 1. *Sobremesa*, I, 1 | Lope, *Selvas y bosques de amor* (Parte XXIV [Zaragoza, 1633], fol. 30) |
| 2. *Sobremesa*, II, 40 | Lope, *El sembrar en buena tierra* (Act I) |
| 3. *Sobremesa*, II, 42 | Lope, *Amar sin saber a quien* (Act III) |
| 4. *Buen aviso*, I, 68 | Lope, *La prueba de los ingenios* (Act II) |
| 5. *Buen aviso*, II, 100 | Rojas Zorrilla, *Obligados y ofendidos* (Act I) |

Unfortunately, however, a large number of these tales appear in so many places that it is impossible to state precisely which source was used by a given dramatist. For example, Buchanan believes the source of no. 5 to have been Melchor de Santa Cruz's *Floresta española* (1574), but the same story had appeared ten years earlier in Timoneda's *Buen aviso*, and again in Lucas Gracián Dantisco's treatise entitled *Galateo español* (ed. Tarragona, 1593, 61v–62r). If it were possible to establish sources on a chronological basis alone, we could conjecture that the story passed from Timoneda to Santa Cruz to Gracián Dantisco to Rojas Zorrilla.

The same difficulty in establishing an exact source obtains with respect to the novel, the other genre that incorporated many anecdotes and motifs that are found in Timoneda's prose fiction. Despite the impossibility of arriving at definitive conclusions, mention must be made here of two novels that have been intensively studied in terms of their analogues and possible sources. One is the *Guzmán de Alfarache* (1599–1604) by Mateo Alemán; the other is *Alonso, mozo de muchos amos* (1624–1626), later called *El donado hablador*, by Jerónimo de Alcalá Yáñez. In the former, for example, there is an important episode (Parte II, Libro III, Capítulo VI) in which the rogue deceives a gentleman into thinking that the latter's fallen money belongs not to the gentleman but to Guzmán. E. Cros and D. McGrady suggest correctly that the incident could have been inspired by a similar tale of Timoneda's (*Buen aviso*, II, 96).[96]

Either as analogues or as possible sources, numerous stories of Timoneda's are related to *cuentos* included in *Alonso, mozo de muchos amos*. J. W. Childers suggests, for instance, that the Valencian's *Buen aviso*, I, 42, on the virtue of silence in preventing marital spats, could have inspired an identical story related by Alcalá Yáñez (Parte I, Capítulo IV).[97]

In short, although specific cases are often difficult to prove, the following comment of Mérimée and Morley describes succinctly the influence exercised by the *Sobremesa*, the *Buen aviso*, and the *Patrañuelo*: "In his turn Timoneda was imitated and even pillaged. He afforded a public supply of stories, anecdotes and witticisms."[98]

CHAPTER 4

# *Theater*

TIMONEDA's keen interest in the theater expressed itself in several forms. He not only did some acting and possibly worked as an actor-manager, but he also edited and published theatrical works of Lope de Rueda, Alonso de la Vega, and Juan de Vergara. It is not surprising, then, that in the third quarter of the sixteenth century, or more exactly between 1558 and 1575, the Valencian bookseller published plays in his own name. These plays belong to precisely the three genres that were to dominate the Spanish stage during the period of its greatest flowering in the seventeenth century: the *entremés*, the *auto sacramental*, and the *comedia*. The *entremés*, or one-act comic sketch, would attain its highest expression in Cervantes and Quiñones de Benavente; the *auto sacramental*, or one-act allegorical Eucharistic play, in Calderón; and the *comedia*, or full-length play, whether "tragedy" or "comedy," in Lope de Vega, Tirso de Molina, and Calderón.

It will be convenient to discuss Timoneda's plays by genre, and in the aforementioned sequence, which shows the relative importance, in ascending order, of the genres rather than of Timoneda's compositions.

In general, Timoneda's plays reflect a theater that is still in its adolescence, not only conceptually and artistically but also from the standpoint of staging. The principal influences on his work are Torres Naharro (c. 1485?–c. 1520), Lope de Rueda (1509?–1565), Italian playwrights like Ariosto, the authors, often anonymous, of *farsas sacramentales* (sacramental farces), and, indirectly, Plautus. Archaic and popular in language, his theatrical compositions with their frequent lack of stage directions and their equally frequent lack of division into acts or scenes, seem to cry out for editing—or for the stage director's instructions—in order to come to life.

## I Entremeses

The four realistic *entremeses* associated with the Valencian bookseller's name form part of a collection entitled *Turiana* that probably appeared in 1565, the latest of several dates found in the volume. The authorship of all ten theatrical compositions in the *Turiana* remains a matter of dispute, for Timoneda, using his anagram Diamonte, in each of the book's seven title pages describes his role with the verb *sacar a luz* (to bring to light, to publish).

Whoever the anonymous author or authors may have been, including Timoneda himself, the works exist today solely in what can be called, at the very least, these *versions* published by the author of the *Patrañuelo*. In the individual titles of the *entremeses* it will be noted that Timoneda uses the names *entremés* and *paso* interchangeably. The compositions will be discussed in the order in which they were printed in the *Turiana*.

### *Entremés de un ciego*

The first of these brief compositions bears the title *Entremés de un ciego y un mozo, y un pobre, muy gracioso* (Very Comic Skit about a Blind Man and a Boy, and a Beggar). Not very promising subject matter for comedy, the modern reader will no doubt think. And indeed in connection with this *entremés* as well as the third one and *patraña* XII, the question does arise as to why the blind—and other physically handicapped persons—provoke laughter (rather than compassion) in medieval and Renaissance audiences. In attempting to answer this complex question, Erik Kraemer draws attention to the following factors:

1. Professional beggars were often guilty of counterfeiting infirmities, thus even legitimate cases caused suspicion.
2. The physically infirm were frequently depicted as having moral defects as well (e.g., the cruel blind man in the *Lazarillo*).
3. The importuning and harassment associated with many beggars created ill will among churchgoers and others.
4. The cruel laughter, or insensitiveness, of those audiences can be correlated with the medieval and Renaissance fondness for public executions and for physically deformed court jesters.
5. From the psychological viewpoint, the spectator laughs at the misfortunes of others out of a conscious feeling of superiority (or an *unconscious* feeling, I might add).

6. Again, psychologically, derisive laughter is produced when one regards the punishment as deserved.[1]

Modern audiences that see comedy in the infirmities of old age should not feel too superior to their ancestors.

As the playlet begins, the blind man is offering to say particular prayers for his prospective clients and is quarreling with, and scolding, his guide Hernando. At the latter's suggestion, the blind man sings to attract customers but his singing is not to Hernando's liking. A crippled beggar appears asking for alms. His plea seems so effective that the blind man fears the competition and so instructs Hernando that they follow him in the expectation of thus driving him away. This leads to an exchange of insults between the blind man and the beggar. When the latter accuses the blind man of being a thief, the blind man tells Hernando to hit him. Here the playlet ends.

Although there are no stage directions, Moratín and others assume that, in the tradition of this genre, the blind man and the beggar engage in an exchange of blows at the play's end.[2]

The fact that the blind man and the beggar are not depicted as sympathetic figures attenuates to some extent the insensitivity inherent in this playlet. The blind man is ill-tempered; he is also a thief if we can believe the beggar. On the other hand, if the blind man speaks the truth, his rival fakes his afflictions.

This first play is written in verse, like all the compositions of the *Turiana*. The predominant meter of the collection is the six-line *copla de pie quebrado*, rhyming *a a b b a a;* the only exceptions being the fifth *paso* and the *Tragicomedia Filomena,* where the *quintilla* predominates.

### *Paso de dos clérigos*

The second playlet bears the title *Paso de dos clérigos, cura y beneficiado, y dos mozos suyos simples* (*Paso* about Two Priests—a Curate and a Chaplain—and Their Simpleton Servants). As the title hints, in this piece the author ridicules the two unworthy priests and their servants. The sketch, which was intended to precede a play, is as follows: The curate advises his servant Juan to be prepared for a fight on account of his dispute with the chaplain. Juan promises to do his duty. The chaplain, meanwhile gives the same advice to his servant Antón, who, though frightened, promises to help. When the two priests meet, they begin to insult each other.

Juan and Antón, in an aside, agree to let their masters do the fighting. As the argument gets heated between the priests over who should receive the various ecclesiastical stipends *(el pie de altar, los responsos, la ofrenda),* Juan unsheathes his sword; at which point, the chaplain runs off, followed by his servant Antón. The curtain-raiser ends as Juan boasts of his bravery and the curate asks for silence so that the play may begin. It should be noted that this is not the only work in which Timoneda calls attention to ecclesiastical shortcomings; the latter is also the subject of an impressive passage in *La oveja perdida* (see below, pp. 85–86).

*Un paso de dos ciegos y un mozo*

The third and best-known of these playlets is entitled *Un paso de dos ciegos y un mozo muy gracioso para la noche de Navidad* (A Very Comic *Paso* about Two Blind Men and a Boy, for Christmas Night). It is a dramatized variant of the story told in Timoneda's *patraña* XII:

The play opens with a lengthy seriocomic monologue in which Palillos, a roguish servant, addresses the audience, telling of his search for a new master and his qualifications. Among the latter, he alleges that he has stolen only once: six ducats from an avaricious blind man who kept him in a state of starvation. But the money is gone, and he needs a master. Martín Alvarez, a blind beggar, appears. He turns out to be the man from whom Palillos stole the six ducats, so the boy hides. Next appears another blind beggar, Pero Gómez, a friend of Alvarez. It is Christmas night and the two blind men offer to say prayers appropriate to the season. Palillos musses their hair; this annoyance they take to be flies. He listens to their conversation. Alvarez explains why he is without his former guide: the boy stole his six ducats. Gómez comments that he keeps his money where it cannot be stolen. He then reveals that he has five to seven ducats hidden in his cap. Whereupon Palillos seizes the cap and flees (as we may assume from the dialogue that follows). Gómez begins to accuse Alvarez of having stolen the cap. Alvarez denies this allegation and the play ends as the two continue to argue about the missing cap.

As in the case of the first playlet, there is no stage direction at the end describing the behavior of the two antagonists. Nonetheless, Moratín[3] and others indicate an exchange of blows, in keeping with both the tradition of the genre and the ending of *patraña* XII.

Whatever the modern reader's reaction may be, the plot of this playlet is at least as old as the medieval French farce *Le garçon et l'aveugle* (1270), according to Crawford.[4] The interlude was imitated in at least two later *entremeses*, according to Cotarelo: *Los ciegos*, attributed to García del Portillo, and *El gato y la montera*, by León Marchante.[5] But, as we have seen in the previous chapter (page 61), Recoules avers that all three *entremeses* derive from Timoneda's *patraña* XII. Leandro Fernández de Moratín (1760–1828), himself a noted playwright, thought enough of this play to edit it in his *Orígenes del teatro español* (1830), and A. Germond de Lavigne translated the playlet into French (1883).[6]

*Paso de un soldado*

Like the preceding curtain-raiser for a Christmas play, the fourth playlet is based on a *burla* (trick). This time the principal victim is a Moor. The play is entitled *Paso de un soldado, un moro y un hermitaño (Paso* about a Soldier, a Moor, and a Monk). A rascally, impoverished soldier appears, boasting of his dubious experiences and abilities. When he spies a Moor who is offering chickens for sale, the soldier immediately plans to trick him. He claims to be the steward of a monastery. At the monastery, the soldier puts his plan to work: in an aside, he tells the Monk that his companion is a penitent who desires confession. The Monk calls out to the Moor to wait a bit and he will take care of him, thus leading the Moor to believe that the Monk will indeed pay for the chickens to be delivered to the "steward." With some reluctance, the Moor gives the chickens to the soldier, who disappears with them at once. The Monk comes out of the monastery expecting to hear a confession while the Moor expects the Monk to pay for the chickens. The Monk soon suspects the soldier's trick but the Moor is not satisfied, continuing to demand payment. In the end, Monk and Moor come to blows in the slapstick tradition of the genre.

This playlet represents an interesting amalgam of elements: the author has grafted the typically Spanish comic types, Soldier, Moor, and Monk, onto a plot of folk or Italian origin. Rotunda, in his *Motif-Index of the Italian Novella in Prose* (p. 89), records the motif in these words: "*Trickster buys chickens telling owner that priest will pay*. When owner comes to collect the trickster tells the priest that a heretic has come for confession. Then he flees" (K 455. 4.1). Two Italian versions are listed: one by Gianfrancesco Straparola (d.

after 1557); the other by Alessandro Sozzini (sixteenth century). Furthermore, according to Cotarelo, this theme was treated in later *entremeses: Los gansos,* anonymous; *Los locos,* anonymous; *Ir por lana y volver trasquilado,* by Bernardo de Quirós; and *La burla del ropero,* by Francisco de Avellaneda.[7] The same investigator also reports a French version of the motif in the farce entitled *Le Nouveau Pathelin* (fifteenth or sixteenth century).

*Paso de la razón*

The fifth play is not comic and therefore does not belong to the tradition of the *entremés.* But since Timoneda calls it a *paso* and since he included it in this group, it will be discussed at this point.

The *Paso de la Razón y la Fama y el Tiempo para la noche de Navidad (Paso* about Reason, Fame, and Time, for Christmas Night) differs from the preceding playlets, not only in its relatively serious content and allegorical style, but also, as noted above, in its predominant meter, which is the *quintilla.* Asensio suggests that it might be more properly called an "allegorical colloquy." According to Crawford (p. 130), the work is "a free imitation of Petrarch's *Trionfi.*" The plot is as follows:

Reason and Fame are maidens; Time is an old man. Reason opens the playlet with the announcement that the Redeemer will soon be born on earth. He will pay for the sin of Adam and Eve. Fame enters, stating that it is her God-given task to record all notable events. Reason and Fame greet each other, the latter declaring herself to be the former's servant. Old Father Time arrives, swiftly moving his wings. Fame complains to him about his destructiveness but he replies that it is his God-given task to undo all that he does. Time and Fame continue to argue until Reason declares them both good, saying that they may both rejoice as this night will be born the Savior of man. The three rejoice and depart, each going his separate way.

Asensio sees little of merit in the satirical plays published by Timoneda.[8] Nonetheless, they deserve consideration as early examples of their genre and for what they reveal about Spanish attitudes toward the types portrayed. Moreover, if the second and the fourth were edited with stage directions, notes on linguistic difficulties, etc., even their "dated" humor could be better appreciated.

## II Autos Sacramentales

In contrast to the brief but realistic and satirical first four *pasos*, Timoneda also cultivated the short *auto sacramental*, which does, however, share the use of allegory and religion with the fifth *paso*. Unlike the latter Christmas play, the *auto*, whether in Timoneda or in later authors, in most cases is related to the sacrament of the Holy Eucharist and the Feast of Corpus Christi.

Among the eight *autos* published by Timoneda is one of his most widely acclaimed works, *La oveja perdida* (The Lost Sheep). The *autos* will be discussed here in the order of their appearance in print, with the exception of one in Catalan *(L' església militant)* and another that is bilingual *(El castell d'Emaús)*, these being treated in Chapter 8.

As in the case of the other genres, the question of the Valencian bookseller's originality arises in connection with these plays, other than *L' església militant*, which, according to its title page, was "compost per Joan Timoneda," and *El castell d'Emaús*, which was "fet per Joan Timoneda" ("done by Juan Timoneda") according to its title page.

In the remaining six cases, Timoneda describes his role with such phrases as "now newly composed and improved by," "newly added to and improved by," "composed and compiled by," "newly composed and added to and improved by," and "perfected by." Other versions of several of the plays have indeed been found. Whether some of these versions are by Timoneda himself (as Juliá Martínez believes)[9] or whether they were written by an author or authors unknown (as other hold), the fact remains that the *autos* as published by Timoneda are revisions that nonetheless deserve to be judged on their own merits.

### *La oveja perdida*

As a printed text, *La oveja perdida* is chronologically the first of Timoneda's *autos;* it is also generally acknowledged to be the best of them. Three early versions of the play exist: a manuscript of uncertain date, a printed version of 1558, and a printed version dated 1575. In the latter edition Timoneda slightly revised his own earlier printed text. But what of the manuscript? According to Pedroso[10] and Wardropper,[11] the manuscript, whoever its author may have been, was the model or source of Timoneda's version. Juliá Martínez, on the other hand, regards the manuscript as a copy or reworking of Timoneda's play.[12] Whatever the truth may be, the Valencian acknowledges that his versions of 1558 and 1575 are *revisions*.

In the following discussion, I shall describe the more accessible version of 1575 as edited in the *Biblioteca de autores españoles*. The play's title page reads as follows: *Auto of the Lost Sheep, a Work Called Pastorela, Newly Revised, Derived from Many Gospels, and Performed in the Presence of the Most Rev. Juan de Ribera, by the Grace of God Patriarch of Antioch and Archbishop of Valencia; and Newly Enlarged by Juan Timoneda.*

The *auto* is preceded by two *introitos* (prologues), one addressed to the archbishop and in praise of him; the second, "for the people," but addressed to the clergy, perhaps, as Pedroso suggests, in representation of the people. The second *introito* indicates the Gospel of St. Luke, Ch. 15, as the chief source of the plot, which is then outlined along with an explanation of the meaning of the allegory. In my summary of the *auto*, I shall indicate in brackets the spiritual meaning of certain characters, events, and objects. The reader should note carefully how the play can be read on the two levels: secular and spiritual. Also to be observed is the Eucharistic element.

The characters in the *auto* are five shepherds—Pedro Preciado [St. Peter], Miguel [Michael the Archangel], Cristóbal Pascual [Christ], Custodio [Guardian Angel], Apetito [Carnal Appetite]—plus Oveja Perdida [Sinful Soul].

As the play begins, Custodio appears with a sheep and is singing to it. The lively animal is almost immediately lured away from Custodio by Apetito, who offers it bread [a reverse allusion to sacramental bread]. Custodio points out that the sheep belongs to Cristóbal Pascual, son of the Head Shepherd, but Apetito claims the animal for his master, Nabuzardán, Head of the *cabrones* (billy goats; also cuckolds). The sheep follows Apetito. Miguel appears and the two begin to search for the lost sheep. They follow the animal's tracks through the following areas, each an allegorical reference to one of the seven capital sins: *Monte Altivo* [Pride], *Codicioso Prado* [Covetousness], *el Vedado del Carnicero* [Lust], *Ejido Airado* [Anger], *Prado de la Golosa* [Gluttony], *Suerte del Pesar del bien ajeno* [Envy], and *Soto de Menga Pérez* [Sloth].

Cristóbal appears, seeking the lost sheep and promising it forgiveness. When Pedro enters, Cristóbal explains why he is willing to leave his ninety-nine to seek the one lost sheep. He also explains to Pedro why he paid such a high price for his flock [allegorical reference to the Crucifixion]. Cristóbal appoints Pedro his shepherd, giving him the keys of the corral and his pastoral leather bag. The latter contains various aids for the flock, each having a symbolic meaning: water [Penance and Baptism], two types of ointment [Confirmation and Extreme Unction], bread and blood [Eucharist] and the Cross, the owner's brand. Cristóbal instructs Pedro on the proper behavior of the true shepherd, insisting on the need for love and forgiveness. Miguel aids Cristóbal and Pedro in the search. Custodio also joins the group. Cristóbal points out that all the sheep has to do to be rescued is cry out. Suddenly, the five shepherds hear the sheep's bleating; they rescue her from a quagmire [sin,], Pedro actually untying, washing, and anointing her [Penance] and finally giving her bread [Eucharist], all as directed by Cristóbal. Joyously, Cristóbal places the sheep on his shoulders and all depart as Custodio sings a Eucharistic song.

The spectator or reader, informed by the *introito* of the play's outcome, is not concerned with dramatic suspense and is therefore free to appreciate the wealth of artistic detail in this lyrical vision of Christ the Good Shepherd. Among the noteworthy aspects of the play are the use of significant names, of songs and probably dance as well, and of modified pastoral speech *(sayagués)*[13] by all the characters. In addition, all three versions (MS, 1558, 1575) include a passage in which Cristóbal sharply but allegorically censures clerical failings:

Sábete que así ha de ser
el verdadero pastor.
   Sabrás que algunos pastores
mejor saben trasquilar
que no, soncas, apriscar,
ni de lobos robadores
a sus ovejas librar.
   Su saber es el cuidado
si las reses se acrecientan,
y es lo peor, ¡mal pecado!,
que no dan pasto al ganado

y a sí mismos apacientan.
  Van a ver la regordida
a la noche y la mañana;
no curan de la transida,
fraca, magra, desmarrida,
pues no da queso ni lana.
(*BAE*, v. 58, p. 85a)

  You should know that thus ought to be
the true shepherd.
  You probably know that some shepherds
know how to shear better
than they know how to gather in the fold, for sure,
or from thieving wolves
to free their sheep.
  Their knowledge consists in care
about whether the animals are increasing
and what is worse, by gosh,
they do not give food to the animals
and they feed themselves.
  They go to see the fat one
by night and day;
they don't care about the paralyzed,
thin, lean, exhausted one
for it gives no cheese nor wool.

It is interesting to note that verse 3 is even stronger in the 1558 edition: "Pero agora los pastores" ("But now the shepherds").

The text of the play includes some stage directions and is written in verse, the predominant meter being the *quintilla*.

*Auto del Nacimiento*

Following *La oveja perdida* in the *Ternario espiritual* of 1558 is a non-Eucharistic play entitled *Auto of the Birth [of Christ], Gloria in Excelsis Deo, a Most Elegant and Excellent Colloquy with Many Questions from Holy Scripture, for Christmas Night. Composed and Compiled by Juan Timoneda from Many and Diverse Catholic Authors.*

The play is preceded by an *introito* in which the interlocutors are the Author and Penca Rucia (gray-haired nag), a simpleton, his servant. The latter asks his master to read for him a letter from his wife Lucia del Otero in which she tells him, among other things, that she has given birth to a child and that she has returned to the curate's service. This upsets Penca Rucia. He has Author write a reply to Lucia, inquiring, among other things, about the baby's sex. Author ends by asking the audience's attention.

The characters in the play are three pilgrims, Solino, Cleonardo, and Polindo, and a shepherd, Tereo.

The play opens as Solino announces the birth of the Savior. Cleonardo and Polindo enter singing a song. They ask Solino many questions about the newborn Christ. In his explanation Solino refers to many Old Testament *types* (prefigurations) of the Virgin birth. The shepherd, Tereo, interrupts the questions and answers in order to report the birth of the Child. It is now Tereo's turn to answer the questions of Polindo and Cleonardo. The Nativity scene appears and the play ends with a Christmas song addressed to the Child and to His Mother.

No source has been found for Timoneda's colloquy, but the Nativity play as a genre has many antecedents among such early Spanish playwrights as Gómez Manrique, Juan del Encina, Lucas Fernández, and Gil Vicente.

Written in *coplas de pie quebrado,* the colloquy is more truly a series of tableaux than a dramatic presentation. The joyous mood of the piece is enhanced by the humor, crude though it may be, of the *introito* and of some of the questions and answers.

The text includes a few stage directions and is followed by a *versión a lo divino* of "Las coplas de Antequera."

### *Auto de la quinta angustia*

Non-Eucharistic like the preceding play, the third and final *auto* of the *Ternario espiritual* of 1558 bears the title *Auto of the Fifth Anguish; a Very Devout and Contemplative Auto on the Descent from the Cross and the Anguish Which the Most Holy Virgin Mary, Mother of God, Suffered at the Foot of the Cross; Newly Composed, Enlarged, and Improved by Juan Timoneda.*

The *introito* is spoken by the prophet Jeremiah, who refers to Christ in typological terms: Isaac, the brazen serpent, Job, Abel, Jacob. He then recites the words of Mary, who reports that Joseph of Arimethea and Nicodemus are approaching.

The play begins as Joseph and Nicodemus discuss aspects of the death of Christ, the former revealing that he intends to ask Pilate for the body. When Joseph speaks to Pilate, the latter requests an account of the death from a centurion, who provides one, indicating his belief that Christ was innocent and the Son of God. Pilate, who feels repentant, grants Joseph permission to remove the body from the Cross and bury it. The Virgin Mary, St. John, and Mary Magdalene lament as the two men remove the body from the Cross, their words strongly suggesting the gruesomeness. Those who accompany the burial, in addition to Joseph and Nicodemus, are the Virgin Mary, St. John, Mary Magdalene, Mary Jacobe (i.e., Cleophas), and probably Mary Salome who appears in the list of "Interlocutores" but is not mentioned in the text. On their way to accompany Mary to her home, all stop at the Cross to adore it. The play ends as Joseph reminds St. John of his responsibility to Mary, adding that St. John should remember him also, for he is one of his flock.

Following the play is a beautiful *villancico* in which the crucified Christ consoles His Mother. In the poem's refrain, He says:

| | |
|---|---|
| Si me adurmiere, madre, | If I fall asleep, mother, |
| no me recordedes vos; | do not awaken me; |
| que si duermo en cuanto hombre, | for if I sleep as a man, |
| siempre velo en cuanto Dios. | I always keep watch as God. |
| (Vol. II, p. 113)[14] | |

There are some stage directions in this play, which is written predominantly in *quintillas*.

The theme of the *mater dolorosa*, traditional in Spanish poetry, appears also in two anonymous plays printed in Burgos in 1552. Whether Timoneda wrote these earlier versions or whether one or the other served as his model remains uncertain. Timoneda's version of 1558 is clearly superior, according to Flecniakoska.[15]

In 1575, under the collective title *Ternario sacramental*, Timoneda published three more *autos:* a slightly revised version of *La oveja perdida*, and the two plays to be discussed in Chapter 8, Works in Catalan-Valencian.

### *Auto de la fuente sacramental*

The same year 1575 saw the appearance of his third collection of *autos: Segundo ternario sacramental* (Second Sacramental Ternary). All three are written in verse, the predominant meter being the *quintilla.* There are few stage directions in the plays, except in the second.

The first of the three Eucharistic plays is entitled *Auto of the Fountain of the Seven Sacraments, in Praise of the Blessed Sacrament and True Body of Our Redeemer Jesus Christ. Improved and Performed before the Most Rev. Juan de Ribera, Patriarch of Antioch and Archbishop of Valencia, by Juan Timoneda. Who Won the Award of Four "Varas" of Crimson Velvet.*

The play is preceded by an *introito* (prologue) and *argumento* (synopsis) recited by the *autor* (theatrical manager). The audience is told that the seven spigots of the fountain represent the seven sacraments. Furthermore, the *autor* urges the public not to seek laughter in the play but rather to contemplate God's gift of Himself in the Eucharist. The characters are Sosiego (Serenity), an old man; St. John (the Apostle), a shepherd; Entendimiento (Understanding), a gentleman; and an Angel.

John appears asking all to celebrate (the feast of Corpus Christi) and declaring that he will keep the unworthy from drinking at the fountain. The Angel appears to John with the message that he must be sure to prevent the unworthy from drinking at the fountain. When the Angel departs, John says he will carefully guard the fountain "do el sin obras y sin fe / se podrá volver sediento"[16] ("whence he who is without [good] works and without faith / will return thirsty"): an interesting reference to the theological controversies of the sixteenth century. Serenity and Understanding arrive at the fountain for the purpose of finding out what one must do to receive the Blessed Sacrament. In answer to Understanding's question, John explains to them why the Eucharist is the greatest of the seven sacraments, as well as other aspects of this sacrament. John insists on the need for faith since the Eucharist is a mystery. He points out that if man cannot understand such a natural phenomenon as the birth and growth of a flower, how can he expect to understand a divine mystery? Serenity asks John to gloss the following five lines: "¿Qué manjar blanco es aquel / tan divino y tan süave? / La Virgen le guisó a él, / de la pechuga del AVE / que le trajo Gabriel"[17] (What white food is that / so divine and so smooth? / The Virgin prepared it / from the breast of the "Ave" [hail; bird] / which Gabriel brought to her"). John does so to the satisfaction of Serenity. John invites the two *faithful* to drink from the fountain and then to declare their feelings. All three praise the Eucharist, enumerating many of the Old Testament prefigurations; the manna of the desert, the Paschal Lamb, the bread given to Elijah by the angel, the banquet of Assuerus, etc. The three burst into exclamations of praise. Serenity and Understanding sing a Eucharistic *villancico* as the play ends.

Thoroughly Eucharistic and almost wholly abstract, this *Auto de la fuente sacramental* lacks the dual-level meanings of such plays as *La oveja perdida*. As the *autor* warned, there is no frivolity here.

It is generally believed that Timoneda's play is a revision of the *Farsa del sacramento de la fuente de San Juan* (Sacramental Farce of the Fountain of St. John), included in the famous *Códice de autos viejos* edited by Rouanet.[18] Whether Timoneda himself wrote the earlier version as Juliá Martínez suggests or whether the sacramental farce must be considered anonymous, Wardropper has shown the many improvements, and alterations (including the elimination of comic material), introduced by Timoneda.

*Los desposorios de Cristo*

The second play of the *Segundo ternario sacramental* is entitled *The Betrothal of Christ, Based on the Gospel of St. Matthew, Ch. 22; Perfected as Much as Possible by Juan Timoneda, the Work Having Been Corrupted on account of Bad Writers.*

The characters are as follows:

Divine King (God the Father), Human Nature (the Bride), Old Testament, New Testament, Adam, Don Juan Menezes (a soldier), the Bridegroom (Christ), Active Life (a maiden), Contemplative Life (a maiden), Lucifer, and Satan.

The play is preceded by an *introito y argumento* addressed to Archbishop Juan de Ribera of Valencia by Juan Timoneda. The poet narrates the parable of the marriage feast as told in St. Matthew, Ch. 22, explaining that the King is God the Father, the Bridegroom is Christ, and the improperly dressed guest is an unrepentant sinner.

As the play opens, Human Nature, dressed as a highland girl, laments her sad state of banishment as a result of her father Adam's disobedience [Original Sin]. Active Life tries to console her. Contemplative Life tells her the King's son will come to be her bridegroom. Old Testament enumerates to the King the Old Testament prefigurations of the marriage of Christ to Human Nature: Esther and Assuerus, Moses and Sephora, etc. The King orders Old Testament to invite the guests and Contemplation to prepare the Bride. He orders New Testament to prepare the Bridegroom. The guests invited by Old Testament [the Jews] do not come so the King orders New Testament to bring in guests [the Gentiles]. New Testament invites everybody. Adam arrives and humbly sits on the ground. The vain, blustering soldier Don Juan Menezes del Canto Pimentel arrives and chooses a good seat. The ill-dressed soldier claims to have fought in Granada, Algeria, Italy, and Lepanto. The betrothal takes place [the Incarnation]. Human Nature asks her Bridegroom to "lift up" her father, Adam, which he does [the Redemption]. The King notices the ill-dressed soldier and orders him thrown out when he refuses, out of pride, to offer any explanation for his appearance. Satan and Lucifer lead him away. (Here the story ends in the parable.) The banquet begins. Bridegroom washes Bride, symbolizing, as the text explains, the sacraments of Baptism and Penance. The courses of the banquet are all symbolic of Christ's suffering and are so explained: the fruit of bitterness, rope, whips, crown of thorns, cross, lance, ladder, and reeds. Finally, Bridegroom offers Himself in the Eucharistic bread. Exclamations of joy follow. The play ends as they sing a short Eucharistic song.

In richness of texture, this *auto*, for which no model or source has been found, ranks with *La oveja perdida*. Timoneda has very effectively grafted his Eucharistic banquet onto the parable whose moral Christ synthesizes in the words "Many are called but few are chosen." In his adaptation of the parable Timoneda carries the lesson a step further so that his play becomes a warning that only those in the state of grace may receive Communion. Also noteworthy in this play is the use of the popular song "Esposo y esposa / son clavel y rosa" ("Husband and wife / are carnation and rose") and the appearance of the swaggering soldier who claims a war record that was very familiar to the Valencian audience.

Typical of Timoneda too is the use of onomastic puns in the Prologue where he refers to Archbishop Ribera with the phrase "ribera fértil" ("fertile shore") and to himself as "un timón con su barquilla" ("a rudder with its boat").

*Auto de la fe*

The third and final *auto* is entitled *Auto of Faith, also Called the Pragmatic Sanction on Bread, Newly Composed in Praise of the Blessed Sacrament, Perfected by Juan Timoneda.*

The play is preceded by an *introito* addressed to the Most Reverend Juan de Ribera, Archbishop of Valencia. The text here suggests that the work was performed by young persons in the service of the Archbishop. The characters are three maidens, Faith, Justice, and Reason, as well as Man, as a simpleton, and World, as a baker.

Faith enters singing a song in which she invites all to take her bread. She then explains that under a new pragmatic sanction God offers to man his body in the bread of the Holy Eucharist provided man is in the state of grace. World then enters singing and offering his bread free. Man appears. Faith and World proclaim the superiority of their respective breads. When Man chooses World's, Faith declares that since he has done wrong, he must be punished. Justice, with a sword, and Reason, with a scale, appear. The latter weighs World's bread and finds it wanting. Whereupon Man repents, declaring his desire to receive the bread of the Eucharist. When Man confesses his guilt and promises to mend his ways, Justice declares him ready to take Communion. World is sentenced to eternal damnation. Man now suggests that Justice, Reason, and Faith join him in a song of praise to the Eucharist that will infuriate World. The play ends with this song, which is essentially a condemnation of the World's bread.

Timoneda's play seems to be a revision of the anonymous *auto* entitled *La premática del pan,* in the *Códice de autos viejos.* Investigators do not agree about the authorship of *La premática:* it may have been written by Timoneda himself or by someone else. After a detailed comparison of the two plays, Wardropper concludes that in the *Auto de la fe* Timoneda corrected stylistic and conceptual errors of the other version.

In this and the other two Eucharistic plays of the *Segundo ternario sacramental,* the spiritual meaning of the allegory so dominates the literal that they can scarcely be read on two levels as is the case with *La oveja perdida.*

In summary, it should be observed that, of Timoneda's eight *autos,* six (including those to be discussed in Chapter 8) are Eucharistic, one is a Nativity play, and one is a Marian play related to Holy Week.

The importance of Timoneda in the development of this genre has been analyzed by Wardropper. By polishing the sacramental farce, elevating its tone and sharpening its theological focus, the Valencian bookseller dignified the genre and prepared it for the achievements of Lope de Vega and Valdivielso. "And in this sense he is the father of the *auto sacramental,*" in Wardropper's words.[19]

## III Comedias

In addition to the *entremés* and the *auto sacramental,* Timoneda also cultivated—after his own fashion—the third great theatrical genre, the *comedia,* or full-length play, whether "comedy," "tragedy" or an amalgam of the two. In recent years, as investigators have come to recognize the importance of Italian influence in the development of the *comedia* of Lope de Vega and his followers, Timoneda's role as a disseminator of that influence has also been correctly assessed.

In 1559 the Valencian published *Las tres comedias del facundísimo poeta Juan Timoneda* (The Three Comedies of the Most Eloquent Poet Juan Timoneda). His purpose, he states in the Prologue, is to offer to the public plays that are (1) in prose, like the successful *Celestina* and *Thebaida,* and (2) brief and stageable, like the verse plays of Torres Naharro and others. Each play is divided into *scenas* (scenes); at the beginning of each scene are found the few stage directions.

### *Comedia de Anfitrión*

The first of the three plays, an adaptation of the famous Plautine comedy *Amphitryon,* deals with a favorite comic subject found in Timoneda's anecdotes, *patrañas, romanceros,* and *cancioneros:* cuckoldry. The full title is *The Play of Amphitryon, Translated and Arranged for Performance by Juan Timoneda. It Contains Very Lofty Sayings and Amusing Incidents* (*pasos*). In the Prologue, the shepherd Morato informs the audience that, in this play originally by Plautus, they will see "especially the vanity with which the pagans adored their gods"; thus Timoneda justifies the presentation of this unexemplary subject matter. Another shepherd, Roseno, provides the background of the play: while the Theban general Amphitryon is away, the enamored god Jupiter, disguised as the general, together with his son Mercury, disguised as Amphitryon's servant Sosia Tardío, arrive at the Theban's home. Here Jupiter makes love to the unwitting Alcumena, Amphitryon's wife. The play's ten scenes may be summarized as follows:

Scenes 1–4: While Jupiter is spending the night with Alcumena, the cowardly Sosia arrives to inform her of her husband's imminent return, but he is prevented from doing so by Mercury. At dawn the two gods depart. When Amphitryon rejoins his wife, he is puzzled by her behavior and decides to seek an annulment of their marriage. Scenes 5–8: During Amphitryon's absence, Jupiter, disguised as the Theban, again deceives Alcumena, while Mercury stands guard outside the house. The son comments that his father wants Amphitryon to be "cornudo y apaleado" (see above, p. 26). The gods leave and Sosia announces that Almucena is about to give birth. Scenes 9–10: Alcumena's maid informs Amphitryon and Sosia that the mistress has borne two sons to the accompaniment of thunder and lightning. In the last scene, Jupiter appears in all his majesty and explains what has happened. The smaller son is Amphitryon's, he says; the larger one is his and shall be called Hercules. Amphitryon is pleased but Sosia is hungry. When the servant informs Mercury that he is from Valencia, Jupiter comments that this fact explains Sosia's fondness for rice. The play ends ironically as all sing a song about jealousy.

Timoneda's statement that he translated this play cannot be accepted too literally. It is generally agreed that the Valencian's comedy is, in Holland Peterson's words, "an adaptation of Dr. Francisco López de Villalobos' *Anfitrion*, Calatayud, 1515, a faithful Spanish translation of Plautus' *Amphitryo*."[20] The same scholar points out that "Timoneda, especially in the short speeches, often copies Villalobos word for word, or nearly so; he shortens the long speeches; he adds to the dialogue puns, proverbs, and many original touches of humour; and he thoroughly hispanizes the *simple*, Sosia. His adaptation, on the whole, shows a good sense of theatre."

Perhaps Timoneda's reference to "translation" has to do with the *cuestión de amor* discussed in the play's Prologue, which is known to have been derived from the first question in the fourth part of Boccaccio's *Filocolo*. The Valencian may have known the original text or he may have used the Spanish translation that was available in several editions.

According to Crawford (p. 124), Cervantes knew Timoneda's Prologue and was influenced by it in his play *La entretenida* (Act III) and in his *entremés*, *La guarda cuidadosa.*

### *Los Menemnos*

Like the preceding play, the second, *Los Menemnos* (The Menaechmi), is an adaptation of a Plautine comedy. Together they constitute the earliest appearance of the great Roman playwright on the Spanish stage. The full title reads: *La comedia de los Menemnos, traducida por Juan Timoneda, y puesta en gracioso estilo y elegantes sentencias* (The Comedy of the Menaechmi, Translated by Juan Timoneda, and Written in Comic Style and Elegant Sayings).

This play, too, involves a favorite motif of Timoneda's, namely, look-alikes, in this case, twins. Three shepherds of the Prologue narrate the background of the story to be unfolded: A rich merchant of Seville has two sons who are identical twins. One named Menemno, after being shipwrecked, comes to Valencia where he eventually marries the only daughter of the wealthy Casandro. (Henceforth he will be referred to as the married Menemno.) The other twin, renamed Menemno in honor of his father and his supposedly dead brother, in searching for his brother, on a fortune-teller's advice, arrives in Valencia with a slave. (Henceforth he will be referred to as the bachelor Menemno). In summary, the plot is as follows:

Scenes 1–4: The married Menemno, accompanied by his father-in-law's witty servant Talega, arranges with his mistress, the prostitute Dorotea, to have a splendid dinner with her at noon. He gives her a skirt belonging to his wife, Audacia. Scenes 5–9: The bachelor Menemno arrives in Valencia with his slave Tronchón, who comments that Valencia is the city of the three R's: *rameras* (prostitutes), *renegadores* (blasphemers), and *regatones* (hucksters). Unwittingly, Dorotea serves the bachelor the dinner she prepared for the married Menemno. She also gives the bachelor the skirt to be fitted and a diamond, belonging to Audacia, to be reset. When the married twin arrives, Dorotea and he quarrel. Scenes 10–13: The bachelor encounters Audacia, Casandro, and Talega; to get rid of them, he feigns madness. Casandro fetches Dr. Averrois, a quack, to cure his supposed son-in-law and indeed, by mistake, the married Menemno is tied up. Tronchón unties him and is granted his freedom. The bachelor appears, permitting the anagnorisis (recognition scene) to occur. In the last scene, the bachelor tells Audacia that his brother will be better behaved in the future and confirms his brother's freeing of Tronchón. The play ends with a brief song.

Concerning the source of Timoneda's adaptation, Holland Peterson states that it "is a reworking of *Menechmos*, Antwerp, 1555, an anonymous Spanish translation of Plautus' *Menaechmi*. A comparison between *Menechmos* and Plautus' version clearly reveals that the Spanish play is a faithful translation. Deviations from the original Latin text may be safely attributed, like those in Villalobos' *Anfitrion*, to the fact that the translator had only corrupt texts at his disposal. It seems likely, however, that *Menechmos* was not Timoneda's only model but that Timoneda, who had at least a smattering of Latin, supplemented it with a Latin text. . . . "[21]

More recently, Sue-Lin Chow has demonstrated that Scenes 3 and 7 reflect the influence of Antonio de Guevara's *Libro áureo de Marco Aurelio* (1529).[22] When we consider that the Prologue of the present play, like that of the preceding one, contains a *cuestión de amor* derived from Boccaccio (*Filocolo*, third question of Part IV), it will be clear that *Los Menemnos* illustrates once more Timoneda's tendency to combine elements from diverse sources into a new structure. In this case he adds zest to the new construct by hispanicizing the setting. Spanish place-names abound: Valencia, el Grao de Valencia, Sevilla, Isla Conejera, Cabo de Cullera, etc. The Spanish audience must have enjoyed the character of Dr. Averrois' servant, Lazarillo, "brother of Lazarillo de Tormes, he who had 350 masters," and a good-natured Valencian audience could laugh at their hometown's being called the city of the three R's.

Finally, this amusing play includes the characters Talega and Tronchón, who bring to mind two types of *graciosos* that will appear in later *comedias*. The former is witty, cowardly, and constantly concerned about food; the latter is knowledgeable, prudent, and clever.

*Comedia llamada Carmelia*

The third of the *Tres comedias* is entitled *Comedy Called* [*Carmelia*],[23] *Newly Composed by Juan Timoneda. It Is Very Eloquent, Amusing, and Joyous.* Complicated in plot, it is the type of play that would be known later as a *comedia de enredo*, or comedy of intrigue. The four characters of the Prologue reveal the following facts that are essential to an understanding of the story: Carmelia is separated at an early age from her father, Lupercio, and later from her secret husband, Taucio. The latter, after the departure of his wife, is also separated from his mother, Poliantea. The play itself is set in Valencia.

Scenes 1–3: Lupercio wishes to marry his son Fulvio to Carmelia, who he thinks is the daughter of a man named Polianteo (in reality, Poliantea, Taucio's mother), but Fulvio is involved in a liaison with Mencía de Logroño, the wife of Cornalla de Pliego, the *simple*, or fool. Scenes 4–7: Taucio and Lupercio seek the aid of a necromancer named Pasquín. This shrewd faker, by piecing together various bits of information, is able to reunite Carmelia with her husband, Taucio, and with her father, Lupercio. He also reunites Taucio and his mother, Poliantea. Futhermore, in the last *scena,* the unsuspecting cuckold Cornalla announces that his wife Mencía has given birth to a son who looks like Fulvio. To cap the climax, the widower Lupercio and the widow Poliantea become engaged. The play ends as all leave the stage singing.

The possible relationship of the role of Pasquín to Ariosto's *Il nigromante* has attracted the attention of several investigators, the latest being Arróniz, who concludes, after a detailed examination, that "Timoneda must have had before him an Italian comedy, a second or third version of Ariosto's *Nigromante,* which he followed to form his."[24] More interesting, from several points of view, than the tangled main plot in which the necromancer plays so vital a part, is the subplot involving Cornalla, Mencía, and Fulvio. Cornalla, whose very name suggests *cuernos,* i.e., the horns of cuckoldry, resembles, as several critics have noted, Martín de Villalba, the contented cuckold of Lope de Rueda's *El deleitoso* (*paso* III). Apparently unnoted, however, is the fact that Timoneda has incorporated into this subplot (Scenes 5 and 6) the erotic anecdote discussed above in Chapter 3, pp. 25–26. In addition, he includes in the Prologue a facetia about Demosthenes and the courtesan Laida that would reappear in the *Sobremesa,* I, 11.

Timoneda's remaining *comedias* appear in the volume entitled *Turiana* (1565), the authorship of which was discussed at the beginning of this chapter. All six compositions are in verse, the *copla de pie quebrado* being the principal meter except in the *Filomena,* where the *quintilla* predominates.

### *Tragicomedia llamada Filomena*

In the *Tragicomedia llamada Filomena* (Tragicomedy Called Philomela) Timoneda brought to the Spanish stage for the first time the story of Tereus, Procne, and Philomela (often "Filomena" in Spanish) told in Book VI of Ovid's *Metamorphoses.* This same tale of revenge would later be the subject of plays, both entitled *Progne y Filomena,* by Timoneda's fellow Valencian Guillén de Castro and by Rojas Zorrilla.

In the Prologue, along with providing a summary of the *ar-*

*gumento* (plot), the *autor* points out to his audience that the play contains laughs but also advice on how to bring up their daughters. The moral, he says, is that unmarried daughters (i.e., like Philomela) should be guarded very diligently. We have here, then, another example of Timoneda's recurrent preoccupation with the morality of pagan literature.

Divided into seven *scenas*, the play can be outlined as follows: Scenes 1–3: King Pandion of Athens reluctantly permits his daughter Philomela to travel with his son-in-law King Tereus back to Thrace to visit her sister, Tereus's wife, Procne. Scene 4: On the way, Tereus rapes Philomela, cuts her tongue to silence her, and abandons her. Scenes 5–7: Philomela is rescued and reunited with her sister, who swears vengeance. She will kill Itys, her son by Tereus, and give him to her husband in his food. In the last scene, upon learning that he has consumed his son, Tereus falls dead. Procne flees with her sister. The play ends with a song which observes that Tereus's filthy and bestial desire cost him his life.

The play moves rapidly from scene to scene like a dramatized *patraña*, always emphasizing action rather than emotion. For example, Procne's decision concerning her son causes her only the most perfunctory grief. One emotion that is not neglected, however, is humor. The playwright promised this quality in his title ("tragicomedy") and in the Prologue. To fulfill the promise, he includes the shepherds Silvestro and Sorato, and especially the *simple* Taurino, whose comic intrusions are constant. Another crowd-pleaser is the use of topical allusions, regardless of their anachronistic character: "vino de la Roda y san Cremente" (p. 68);[25] "el puerto de Denia," "la villa de Alarcón" (p. 87), etc.

As noted in Chapter 3, page 66, the Procne-Philomela story and the consumed-son motif appear elsewhere in Timoneda's works. Furthermore, a Spanish translation of Ovid's masterpiece is listed in the 1583 Inventory of Timoneda's bookshop.[26]

### *Farsa llamada Paliana*

Concerning the second play, entitled *Farsa llamada Paliana* (Farce Called Paliana), Crawford, in agreement with Moratín, says: "It has not a single redeeming quality" (p. 128).

The author states in the Prologue that the play is about a dream, "a vain thing / as will be seen later." Then, confirming his use of the label "farce," he adds that, although it is not sententious, the play is very funny because, he tells the audience, "that's what you most enjoy."

The play itself is not divided into acts or scenes and includes almost no stage directions. As indicated, the main plot centers on a dream. Paliano's pregnant wife, Filomancia, dreams that flames issue from her womb, that these flames are extinguished by two *salvajes* ("wild men") and that the fire turns to pleasure. Doctor Tolomeo, a necromancer who lives on Carrer Mayor near la Seo (Valencian toponyms), interprets the dream to mean that Filomancia will bear a son whose ardors will endure "until two *salvajes* / are caught in a mountain." He advises the parents to abandon the child, adding that Paliano will one day wish to kill the boy but should not do so. The baby boy is abandoned but is rescued by two *salvajes*. At the play's end, some twenty years later, Paliano recovers his wife, *unharmed*, from the two *salvajes* and the boy who unwittingly fell in love with Filomancia. Parents and son are reunited. There is a song and the play ends.

In this absurd plot are folk motifs that were to appear again in the *patrañas:* the prophetic dream and exposure of the baby; dream fulfillment, near mother-son incest. But, in keeping with the Prologue's promise, the author has interspersed a number of comic incidents, or *pasos*, among them: pp. 107–110,[27] Paliano tries to give orders to a dull-witted worker named Juan Sano who is more interested in eating; pp. 110–111, Paliano scolds his sleepy steward, Albero; pp. 130–131, the Devil tries to persuade Juan Sano to commit suicide; pp. 138–140, an amorous Portuguese tries to woo the servant, Belisena; etc. If the play has any "redeeming quality," it is the presence of these comic episodes, but, all in all, the farce is an unsuccessful mix of too many ingredients.

### *Comedia Aurelia*

The next play is divided into five *jornadas* (acts) with accompanying lists of characters. The structure of this play, entitled *Comedia Aurelia,* has been aptly described by Crawford: "The exposition is given in the first act, the *dénouement* in the fifth, and the interval is filled up with wholly irrelevant matter" (p. 128). The author's intention, according to the Prologue, is "esquivar pasos de amores / y tomar nueva invención" ("to avoid matters of love / and to use a different fiction").

In Act I, the parents of Saluzio and Aurelia have died, leaving them in poverty. Saluzio reveals to his sister their father's deathbed secret: prior to his children's birth, he arranged with a necromancer to hide his great wealth in a tower. The key to the tower is a ring, half of which Saluzio now has, while the other half was thrown into the sea, thus causing the tower to become invisible. Why the second half of the ring was thrown into the sea is never explained but, not surprisingly, it has not been recovered. Act V opens with a song sung by two pilgrims, Sipariso and Gandino, whom Saluzio meets in a forest. Sipariso has a half-ring that the pilgrims found in a fish. The two halves are matched and to the accompaniment of a loud noise, the treasure becomes visible. Aurelia and Sipariso become engaged and the play ends joyously.

No source has been found for this fantastic plot, but its relationship to the common motif known as "identification by ring" has been suggested. This motif is found in Timoneda's *patraña* IX and in the latter's possible partial source, Sabadino degli Arienti's *Le porretane, novella* 22, where the identifying ring is recovered from inside a fish.

The "irrelevant matter" to which Crawford refers involves the humorous characters that the author introduces, no doubt to make the fantasy more palatable. These comic types include: Ginebra García, Aurelia's sleep-loving housekeeper; the equally lazy *bobo*, or simpleton, Lucas (Luquillas); a Portuguese; a Basque; a Castilian Soldier; a Frenchman; Pabros Cremente, an old gardener; his son, Juan, another *bobo;* two gypsy men, Perogordo and Alonso; and a nameless gypsy woman. The resulting mix of ingredients is an ineffective hodgepodge.

The author's clearly demonstrable debt to Torres Naharro in this play has been detailed by Gillet.[28]

*Farsa llamada Trapacera*

The next play bears the title *Farsa llamada Trapacera sacada a luz por Joan Diamonte* (A Play of Deceits Brought to Light by Juan Diamonte). The Prologue advises that the work is written in the Italian manner but does not point out that it is an abridged, very close adaptation of Ariosto's play *La Lena*.

Not only are there no indications of act or scene division and no stage directions, but two folios (45 and 54) are missing in the unique extant copy.

The plot is essentially the same as Ariosto's. The setting, however, is no longer Ferrara, but Valencia. Flavio, Hilario's son, goes to an assignation with Licea, Facio's daughter, in the house of the unscrupulous Rufina, who is supposedly teaching the girl to sew. Later, to avoid discovery, Flavio is forced to hide in a wine cask that is then sent, with him in it, to Facio's house, to remain on deposit until a dispute over its ownership can be settled. Dominica, Facio's servant, reports to him that she has seen Flavio and Licea in an embrace. Facio is furious at being thus dishonored in his own house. As Hilario tries to calm him, the play is interrupted by a missing leaf. In Ariosto, however, the comedy ends with the reconciliation of the fathers and the engagement of the lovers.

G. Ledda, after showing how the Valencian hispanicized and popularized the Italian original, declares: "Ariosto had performed a first act of mediation between the Plautine theater and the Ferrarese setting; Timoneda carries out a second one between literary work and public, he achieves a comedy that possesses greater sprightliness, developing easily without entanglements, slack moments, or erudite quotations" (p. 164).[29]

*Farsa llamada Rosalina*

The last complete play of the *Turiana* is entitled *Farsa llamada Rosalina muy apacible y graciosa, agora nuevamente sacada a luz por Joan Diamonte* (Play Called Rosalina Very Pleasant and Humorous, Now Newly Presented by Juan Diamonte). The Prologue calls attention to the moral lesson to be learned from this play, viz., "how to forget the world." There are no indications of scene or act division nor are there any stage directions. The main plot is simple. Two widowers, Leandro and Antonio, decide to enter the religious life. Lucano, Leandro's father-in-law, is to assume the responsibility of marrying off Rosalina, the widower's daughter. The two former merchants are not dissuaded from their purpose by brief encounters with Devil, World, and Flesh. In the end, Lucano sends the agreeable Rosalina to a convent and he, too, enters a monastery. Interspersed with this plot, whose dramatic potentialities are not developed, the author includes much crowd-pleasing material of the usual sort: a Portuguese who is doused with water when he claims to be burning with love for Rosalina, two bickering servants, etc.

*Farsa llamada Floriana*

Of the *Turiana's* final play, *Farsa llamada Floriana* (Farce Called

Floriana), only two folios have survived, the first one and the last. From the list of characters it can be inferred that this play was another amalgam of fantasy and comedy. The characters include: a sacristan (not seen previously in Timoneda), an old shepherd, his simpleton son, a nymph, two satyrs, a merchant, his daughter, a simpleton, a blind man, a serving-girl, a page, a knight, an old go-between, a Portuguese, and an Italian necromancer!

In the development of the Spanish *comedia*, Timoneda played an important role as a popularizer. In the words of Froldi: "The recognition that Timoneda gave in Valencia to the literary validity of Lope de Rueda's theater, after his success with the public, has a strict historical significance, because it signals the advent of a new genre, free of the restrictions of classical literary models or the conventions of academic settings, and determined, instead, on an effective effort at communication with an extensive circle of listeners."[30]

More recently, J. M. Regueiro, author of the doctoral dissertation entitled "Juan Timoneda y la tradición dramática española" (1972), has aptly described the importance of Timoneda's theater in the following terms:

> In his adaptations of the Plautine and Italian comedies to the Spanish stage and to the tastes of the emerging popular audiences, Timoneda displays much dramatic skill and ingenuity. In his shorter pieces, the Valencian author prefers to focus the main interest in developing vivid and agile dialogues, particularly those of the *bobos* and *simples*.
>
> We view the formation of the *comedia* and the *auto sacramental*, the two dramatic genres peculiar to the Spanish soil, rather than as the result of the creative genius of one single dramatist, as the product of the cumulative achievement of many dramatists who shaped a multisecular tradition, religious and profane, to adapt it to the popular taste of the mid-sixteenth century audience. Timoneda is an important member of this generation of dramatists who in this period bring old and new themes to the stage, making them appealing to the *vulgo,* whose dictates will dominate the Spanish theater for the next hundred years.[31]

CHAPTER 5

# *Poetry*

IN this chapter will be examined Timoneda's important activity as a poet and an anthologist of poems. Following a practice common in his era, the Valencian bookseller assembled and published a considerable number of anthologies of anonymous poems. The authorship of most of these compositions is not known and possibly may never be discovered. Nor is it known in most cases whether or not Timoneda himself composed any of them. For these reasons, when we speak of a given work as Timoneda's poem, what is actually meant is Timoneda's *version* of the poem in question. Antonio Rodríguez-Moñino, whose name will appear frequently in the present chapter on account of his great contributions to our knowledge of this subject, stated that "the compiler [of this type of poetic anthology], whether or not he is the author of any of the assembled compositions, feels himself to be responsible for the ensemble which represents his esthetic taste or his ability as a researcher."[1] As for Timoneda's refashioning of earlier poems, the same scholar gives the following dramatic example of what he calls the Valencian's "poetic carpentry": "The [ballad] that begins 'Ricas bodas Macenisa,' in its original edition [Alonso de Fuentes, *Cuarenta cantos*, Seville, 1550] is composed of eighty-four verses, which [in Timoneda's *Sarao de amor*] have been reduced to fifty-two, that is, no fewer than thirty-two are eliminated from various places; but, in summarizing, at times he condenses eight verses of the original into two and twenty into four. Eight octosyllables are rewritten so that the omissions will not interrupt the text."[2]

It will be convenient to describe and analyze Timoneda's poetic compilations in the following chronological order: *Sarao de amor* (1561), *Flor de enamorados* (1562), *Villete de amor* (1565?), the several *cancionerillos* of 1573, the four *Rosas de romances* of 1573, and, as a final unit, the shorter, miscellaneous *pliegos sueltos*, or chapbooks, which, in certain cases, may actually be chronologically older than some of the above collections.

Timoneda, always methodical if not inspired, gives structure to his collections by separating the compositions into groups, each with its own heading or title. Sometimes the inclusion of a given poem in a given category may be capricious; at times the heading is merely an indication of metrical form, but in other cases, the Valencian's heading provides important orientation as will be noted below.

## I Sarao de amor

Timoneda's earliest extensive anthology *Sarao de amor* (Soirée of Love) was printed in 1561 by the noted Valencian printer Joan Navarro. Of this two-part compilation, which has never been reprinted, only one copy is known to exist. The unique octavo exemplar in the Biblioteca Nacional of Madrid, though badly mutilated, consists of some 175 compositions, the majority of which deal, as the title suggests, with love. All of Part I has been lost except for the final poem of a section of ballads, plus a group of thirty sonnets whose heading reads: "There follow many sonnets by different authors. And this first one was written by the author [Timoneda] in praise of all those that follow." The single ballad, "Entre muchos reyes sabios," about King Búcar, was reprinted in Timoneda's *Rosa de amores* (1573 and 1574), in keeping with the bookseller's practice of reusing material he liked or that he thought would sell. In the first sonnet, Timoneda says with humorous modesty that he deliberately mixed poems by other unidentified authors with his own sonnets so that the great merit of the others' works would enhance his own.

The difficulty of determining the identity of the authors of the other twenty-nine sonnets is illustrated by Rodríguez-Moñino, who states that the twenty-third poem, "Riberas del Danubio al mediodía," has been attributed elsewhere to Ramírez Pagán, don Diego Hurtado de Mendoza, Luis de Camoëns, and Hernando de Acuña.[3] As will be noted in Chapter 8, this section includes a "Sonnet in Seven Languages" (Latin and six Romance tongues) and a "Sonnet on the Death [in 1558] of Our Emperor Charles the Fifth, in Two Languages" (Castilian and Valencian-Catalan). The extant compositions of Part II are grouped in six well-defined categories. Group 1 consists of some forty-nine songs in which *el galán* (lover [male]) and *la galana* (lover [female]) sing alternately of their love, or two *amigos* (friends [male]) discuss the subject of love. In structure, the songs are either *canciones* or *villancicos*.

As these two genres play so important a role in Timoneda's anthologies, it will be well to examine them here in some detail. Both consist of a relatively short introductory stanza or refrain and a gloss, with the difference that the refrain of the *canción* is composed of four or more verses, whereas the *villancico*'s refrain contains three or fewer verses. The gloss (*glosa* in Castilian; *glossa* or *glosse* in Catalan), as the name implies, expands on the theme of the opening stanza. The introductory stanza, which will be called the refrain throughout this book, is called in Castilian *estribillo, cabeza, pie*, or *villancico-núcleo;* in Catalan, *refrany*. Because of their spontaneous, popular flavor, these refrains have attracted considerable attention from scholars in recent years. There is reason to believe that many of them derive from, or at least are imitations of, popular folksongs, a fact that explains why the same refrain, with minor or major variations, appears in numerous compositions by different poets in different periods. As Margit Frenk Alatorre says, speaking of these recurrent elements, "They prove that at least a part of the popular-type songs that Renaissance and post-Renaissance sources offer us were true folksongs, a fact questioned by some investigators. Not all are pastiches, nor merely 'popularizing' poems. On the other hand, there can be no doubt, and we must always keep it in mind, that many popular-type songs were colored, modified, re-created, if not created, by the authors that have transmitted them to us: the popular-type lyric of that period lies halfway *between folklore and literature*."[4]

This folk or traditional-type element may be, and often is, combined with a more cultivated or erudite current, that of courtly love. Of the latter phenomenon perhaps no better analysis can be found than the following words of Otis Green as he describes the influence of this concept in Spain:

> . . . the memory of the medieval dream of love is in some form almost always present to the very end of the Renaissance. Every writer knows that love is (or has been thought to be) ennobling, the business of courteous and gentle hearts; that it is born of the contemplation of a beautiful woman; that suffering for its sake is (or has been thought to be) blessed; that the beloved, by the mere fact that she is desired and not desiring, is superior to the lover who, in his longing for her perfection, is himself imperfect; that desire is the essence of love; that the intensity of this desire may cause the lover to 'deify' his lady; and finally that such a love will always be viewed by the rigorists as unholy, a *truancy*, a departure from the prosaic world of the permitted into the infinitely enticing world of the disallowed—a truancy from which a

return must be made, either through marriage and acceptance of responsibility, or through the poetic device of the warning . . . and the palinode. . . . These ideas, though subject to change and distortion, retain for centuries at least some portion or vestige of their validity. They are present, in fully developed or in adumbrated form, in practically all the literature that in any way involves the amorous passion, from the earliest lyric poem in Castilian to Calderón (d. 1681).[5]

With regard to the distribution of their personae, Timoneda's *canciones* and *villancicos* fall mainly into three classes: (1) the *galán, galana,* or *amigo* speaks in one poem called the *pregunta* (question, stimulus, cue) and is answered in another called the *respuesta* (response); or (2) the speaker's poem is a separate unit; there is no response; or (3) each poem is constructed as a dialogue, usually between two conventionalized pastoral figures.

Following is an example of the duet-type *canción.* In both poems, the refrain and the gloss are written in octosyllables, the third and fourth verses of the refrain being repeated in the seventh and eighth lines of each stanza of the gloss. The courtly attitude toward amorous suffering should also be observed.

*Canta el galán:*
Aguila que vas volando
lleva en el pico estas flores;
dáselas a mis amores,
dile cómo estoy penando.
Lleva flores a la flor
de mi salud y dolencia,
y con salva real de amor
saludarás su presencia.
Mis encomiendas llegando
cual te diré, sin temores
dáselas a mis amores
dile cómo estoy penando.
Y si ignoras quién es ella,
sólo en mirar su lindeza
perderás la vista en vella
que te dio naturaleza.
Las fuerzas destar mirando
el sol, mundo y sus primores,
dáselas a mis amores
dile cómo estoy penando.

*The gallant sings:*
Eagle that goes soaring
carry in your beak these flowers;
give them to my beloved,
tell her how I am suffering.
Carry flowers to the flower
of my health and illness,
and with royal salute of love
you will greet her presence.
Bearing my regards
as I shall tell you, without fear
give them to my beloved,
tell her how I am suffering.
And if you don't know who she is,
only in gazing on her beauty
you will lose your vision in seeing her
that Nature gave to you.
The strength to be looking at
the sun, the earth, and its beauties,
give it to my beloved
tell her how I am suffering.

Dirásle la pena fuerte
que de su parte me guarda,
y cuán cierta m[e] es la muerte
si el remedio mucho tarda.
Si de mí se va acordando,
las mercedes y favores
dáselas a mis amores
dile cómo estoy penando.
(fol. 13r–v)

*Responde la galana:*

Vuelve, águila, a volar
al galán que a mí te envía,
dirásle de parte mía
que quien sirve ha de penar.
Vuelve por donde viniste,
ante mí no te detengas,
sino que vayas y vengas
para consolar al triste.
Y con tu gentil mirar,
como de ti se confía,
dirásle de parte mía
que quien sirve ha de penar.
Vuelve, águila, de presto
pues de ti quiso servirse
qu'en tardar podrá morirse
y serás tú causa desto.
Y por más le consolar
que prosiga en su porfía
dirásle de parte mía
que quien sirve ha de penar.
Vuelve, mis dichos se atajen,
y dile, si te parece,
que gloria no se merece
sin que por ella trabajen.
Sufra si quiere gozar,
y si ignorancia acogía
dirásle de parte mía
que quien sirve ha de penar.
(fol. 13v–14r)

You will tell her the strong pain
that comes to me on her account,
and how certain is my death
if the remedy is too long in coming.
If she does give thought to me,
the graces and favors
give them to my beloved
tell her how I am suffering.

*The lady replies:*

Return, eagle, and fly
to the gallant who sends you to me,
you will tell him for me
that he who courts must suffer.
Return to where you came from,
in my presence do not stay
but rather go and come
to console the sad one.
And with your gentle gaze,
as he confides in you,
you will tell him for me
that he who courts must suffer.
Return, eagle, quickly
since he wished to use your services
for with your delay he may die
and you will be the cause of this.
And to console him more
let him continue in his persistence;
you will tell him for me
that he who courts must suffer.
Return—let my words be brief—
and tell him, if you like,
that glory is not deserved
without an effort being made for it.
Let him suffer if he wishes to enjoy,
and if he was ignorant of this
you will tell him for me
that he who courts must suffer.

Typical of the casuistry of love that characterizes these songs is another exchange (fols. 18v–19v) that begins when the gallant sings, "I shall die, if you so wish, / my lady, in good faith / of love I shall die." After he expands on this theme in three stanzas, the lady replies, "Never did I see dead from love / any faithful lover; / on account of love, yes sir, I did." She proves her point in the subsequent strophes by citing the examples of Leander, Pyramus, Acteon, Calisto, Paris, and Agenor. One poem of this group is entirely in Valencian; another is all Valencian except the first three verses, which are in Castilian. Eight of these songs reappeared as the first selections of the *Cancionero llamado Dança de galanes*, compiled by Diego de Vera (Lérida: [Luys Manescal], 1612). Group 2 comprises a similar body of thirty-six *canciones* and *villancicos*, but here they are individual works, rather than exchanges wherein replies are essential. Among the outstanding poems of this section are the twentieth, a *canción* in which the lover asks his beloved *morena* (brunette or swarthy-skinned girl) to lower her eyes for they wound him, and the last, a *villancico* in which a *bella malmaridada* (a beautiful but unhappily married woman) laments her plight. Three of the songs of this section are in Valencian.

Group 3 is composed of fourteen *canciones* and *villancicos* written "a modo pastoril" (in the pastoral manner). Typical of several poems in dialogue is the first *canción*, whose refrain reads as follows:

| | |
|---|---|
| —Gil, no seas enamorado, | —Gil, don't fall in love, |
| que va en perdición tu vida. | for your life is in danger. |
| —A la mía fe, Juan Collado, | —By my faith, John Hill, |
| quien bien ama tarde olvida.[6] | he who loves well forgets late. |

When John asks Gil how he can love a woman who doesn't love him, Gil, a courtly lover in shepherd's clothing, points out that if his beloved did love him, he would be "doing little in loving her."

The third poem of this group is a sort of amorous pastoral parody of the "ubi sunt" theme as seen in Jorge Manrique's "Coplas por la muerte de su padre," vv. 181 ff. Here are the refrain and the first stanza of the gloss:

| | |
|---|---|
| ¿Qué son de tus gallardías, | What has become of your gallantries, |
| Mingo ha, | oh Mingo, |
| que no te quillotras ya | for you no longer fall in love |
| como solías? | as you used to. |
| Aquel peinar de cabello | That combing of your hair, |
| —dime Mingo— | tell me, Mingo, |
| y el luchar, bailar, respingo, | and the wrestling, dancing, leaping, |

| | |
|---|---|
| ¿qué fue dello? | what's become of it? |
| Tu tañer de gaiterías, | Your playing, all dressed up, |
| ¿dónde está? | where is it? |
| Que no te quillotras ya | For you no longer fall in love |
| como solías.[7] | as you used to. |

Also worthy of note is the *canción* that begins "Three mountain girls I met," which, as Arthur Terry suggests, is a refashioning of the famous poem by the Marqués de Santillana (1398–1458), "A sus fijas, loando la su fermosura."[8]

Group 4 bears the heading "Here begin many new and comic riddles." Having completed his section of *canciones* and *villancicos* "in the pastoral manner," Timoneda continues in this vein by devoting several folios to a genre associated in Spanish literature with the life of shepherds and shepherdesses. The verse riddle appears in such famous pastoral novels as *La Diana enamorada* (1564), Book V, by Timoneda's fellow Valencian Gaspar Gil Polo, and in *La Galatea* (1585), Book VI, by Cervantes. Representative of Timoneda's unsophisticated riddles is the fourth one, which asks "why a dog enters the church and goes out again." The answer: "because the door is open." Following the twenty riddles are four *juegos de ingenio* (ingenious trifles or games of wit), the last of which is described as "Three verses made with such artifice that they read the same backwards as forwards." The three palindromes are: "Ola moro moro malo / No tardes y sed ratón / No deseo ese don."

In Group 5 Timoneda returns to the ever popular ballad form to offer his readers fourteen "Ballads of illustrious and crowned women of notorious fame, both Greek and Roman, and of other nations. . . ." The poems deal with the following celebrated women in this order: 1, Hippo; 2, Tymbria; 3, Emilia; 4, Sophonisba; 5, the wives of the Teutons and Cimbrians; 6, Cloelia; 7, Leaena; 8, Penelope; 9, Argia; 10, Iole; 11, Cleopatra; 12, Alcione; 13, Marcia; and 14, Lucretia. In his characteristic way, Timoneda reprinted numbers 1, 2, 3, 4, 5, 6, 8, 9, 13, and 14 in his *Rosa gentil* of 1573 and number 11 in his *Rosa de amores* of 1573. Of the three not reprinted, perhaps the most interesting is number 10, which tells the story of Iole, who, forced to marry Hercules, the man responsible for her father's death, avenges her father by pretending to love Hercules and by persuading him to adopt female clothing and ways, including the telling of *patrañuelas* about his past life.

A check of Rodríguez-Moñino's *Manual bibliográfico de cancioneros y romanceros (siglo XVI)* reveals that numbers 1, 2, 3, 6, 7, 8, 9, 10, 11, and 12 appear only in Timoneda's collections.[9] On the other hand, the stories of all but numbers 12 and 13 are told in Boccaccio's *De Claris Mulieribus* (written 1355–1359), the first collection of biographies exclusively of women.

The final group of poems comprises compositions that involve the artificial devices of anagrams and acrostics. In the first poem, Timoneda advises that "nine ladies' names are inserted." The first eight appear when the last word of the uneven verses is joined to the first word of the even lines. The last or ninth name is an acrostic of the initial letter of the uneven verses. Next, the compiler says, "Here follow many *canciones* and *villancicos* made with such artifice that in the first line of each is enclosed the name of a lady." Only the following six *villancicos* have survived, the lady's name here indicated in italics:

1. Bien hace *y sabe el* amor [Isabel]
2. Traba*jo ha na*cido en veros [Juana]
3. Sois *león, or*o también [Leonor]
4. Consue*lo y sa*lud me dais [Luisa]
5. De aqu*el en a*quel pasea [Elena]
6. *Amaría na*vegando [Mariana]

For the charm of its love lyrics, the humor of its verse riddles, and the insight it gives into popular literary taste in Renaissance Spain, Timoneda's *Sarao de amor* deserves to be reprinted. Although such traditional forms as the octosyllabic ballad, the *canción*, and the *villancico* clearly predominate in the *Sarao*, the anthology shows that by the 1560's the hendecasyllabic sonnet was also considered suitable for popular consumption.

## II Flor de enamorados

In 1562, the year following the appearance of the *Sarao de amor*, the Barcelona printer Claudi Bornat issued a similar *Cancionero llamado Flor de enamorados, sacado de diversos autores ahora nuevamente por muy linda orden copilado* (Songbook Entitled Flower of Lovers, Gathered from Different Authors Now Newly Arranged in Very Attractive Order).[10] This earliest known edition of the famous bilingual anthology does not include a compiler's name, as do later printings, which name a totally unknown "Juan de Linares." In the last few years, however, two Catalan scholars, Josep Romeu i Figueras[11] and Joan Fuster,[12] have argued convincingly that the compiler of the *Flor de enamorados* (Flower of Lovers) was our Valencian bookseller Juan Timoneda. Their arguments in favor of Timoneda can be summarized as follows: first, the Catalan-language selections show Valencian influence; second, many compositions are linked to such Valencian poets as Juan Fernández de Heredia, Luis Milán, Francisco de Castelví, and Timoneda himself; third, and most important, in a recently rediscovered document dated January 27, 1556, Juan Lorenzo de Villarrasa, Governor and Captain-General of Valencia, granted Timoneda a license to publish "a book entitled *Flower of Lovers*, distributed in two volumes, that is, in a first and second part."

Printed in small duodecimo, the *Flor* consists of some 280 compositions mostly amorous in nature, which, like those of the *Sarao*, are distributed in two parts containing well-defined categories. The categories of Part I correspond very closely to those of Part II, as will be observed below.

Like Part II of the *Sarao*, Part I of the *Flor* opens with a group of *canciones* and *villancicos* in which the *galán* and *galana* sing alternately to each other. Of these fifty-four poems, twenty-six are in Castilian; twenty-eight, in Catalan. The exchanges are linguistically very flexible: a Castilian poem may be answered in that language or in Catalan; a Catalan poem may be answered in Catalan or in Castilian. Group 2 consists of thirty-one *canciones* and *villancicos* but in this case they are individualized, that is, without the replies of Group 1. Only one of these poems is in Catalan. The Valencian origin of the anthology is reflected in the fourth poem of this section, a *villancico* whose refrain reads: "Let the tears of my heart / pour and pour from my eyes / for they have every reason to." The cause of the lover's tears is a maiden who is "the flower of flowers / of those that are in Valencia."

Among the refrains that seem to be of popular origin is the one that says, "My love is going away / he wishes to leave me; / although I am swarthy *(morena)*, / I'm not easy to forget." Another example of the well-known "morena" theme, these verses appear with a different gloss in the *Cancionero sevillano de la Hispanic Society* (c. 1568) and in the *Arte de la lengua* (1625) of Gonzalo Correas. Section 3 is devoted to a poem of six stanzas entitled "Very Comic Fortune of a Gypsy Woman to Be Told to Any Gallant."

Thereafter is inserted the oldest known secular version of the celebrated poem that begins "If Antequera is won / would that it were Granada," which deals with the love of a Moorish girl and a Christian soldier. Timoneda himself had published a spiritualized version of the same poem at the end of his *Auto del Nacimiento* (Nativity Play) in 1558; see Chapter 4, p. 87. In the following very brief section, the compiler returns to the subject of fortune-telling but now in a more serious vein; for instance, the first *mote* says, "Your fortune and mine / ask it only of God / who knows that of both of us." Section 5 is devoted to twenty-one verse riddles, like those in the fourth section, Part II of the *Sarao de amor* (Soirée of Love). In this case, though, the compiler includes an obscene acrostic (fol. 45r).

Section 6 bears the compiler's rubric "Here begin the very eloquent ballads of love." Despite this heading, not all sixteen ballads deal with romantic love: the "Ballad of Don García" describes a ruse by which this knight caused the Moors to lift their siege of his castle; the "Ballad of the Cid" concerns the test to which the Cid's father submitted his three sons in order to determine which one should avenge him. According to Romeu i Figueras, seven of the sixteen ballads are old and traditional. Striking too is the fact that Timoneda reprinted twelve of these sixteen ballads in his *Rosas de romances* of 1573, the only ones not reprinted by the Valencian being those that begin: "A la qu'el sol se ponía," "En aquellas peñas pardas," and "Atal anda don García." The ballad "Amores trata Rodrigo" also appears in the *Rosa de amores,* but in a version different from that of the *Flor.* It is Romeu's belief that seven of the sixteen ballads were composed by Timoneda (p. 68).

Section 7 is composed of four *lamentaciones,* three *chistes,* and two *endechas.* The four *lamentaciones,* in verses of eight and four syllables, are amorous laments. Also in verses of eight and four syllables, the three *chistes* (witticisms) express various moods of the lover: pride, joy, anger. In the two *endechas* (dirges) the poet-lover gives vent to his despair, in the first poem using verses of six syllables, in the second one using verses of eight and four syllables. The first dirge, "Parióme mi madre" (My Mother Bore Me) is especially well known and includes an astrological reference that many modern readers would appreciate.

The last section of Part I consists of two sonnets on the widely diffused theme of Hero and Leander. The first, "Pasando el mar,

Leandro el animoso," is one of a considerable number of the *Flor's* compositions whose authors have been identified with some degree of certainty. This particular sonnet, by the celebrated Garcilaso de la Vega (1501?–1536), appeared often in the sixteenth century; Timoneda himself gives the original and a spiritualized version in one of his undated chapbooks. The second sonnet, "Hero del alta torre, do miraua," is anonymous and also found in other collections.

Part II begins with a section described as follows in the rubric: "There follow other different replies and questions of lovers of the same type." The compiler refers to the same type of *canciones* and *villancicos,* in which gallant and lady sing alternately, that make up the first section of Part I. In this case there are sixty-four compositions, of which forty-two are in Castilian and twenty-two in Catalan. Moñino and Devoto as well as Romeu have commented on the popular flavor given to the *Flor* by the frequent appearance of proverbial expressions; for example, in this section a lady dismisses her lover with the words: "Say good-bye to that flame / because *in the nests of yore / there are no birds this year* / nor love in the one who no longer loves you / because, so help me, / however much you may be insistent / *I comb not my hair for you* / nor do I care at all for you" (fol. 75r). The first expression was used very effectively by Don Quijote not long before his death *(Don Quijote,* II, Ch. 74).

As in Part I, the second section of Part II is composed of *canciones* and *villancicos,* each of which is a separate poem, having no reply. Of the twenty-four compositions, one is actually a ballad with a refrain. All are in Castilian except for three in Catalan and one bilingual *canción.* The best known poem of this group, "Bella, de vós só enamorós" ("Beautiful, I'm in love with you"), is not in Castilian and will therefore be discussed in Chapter 8 (Works in Catalan-Valencian).

Sections 3, 4, and 5 correspond exactly to the same sections of Part I, containing, in this order: one "Fortune of a Gypsy Woman," six *motes,* and fourteen verse riddles, all twenty-one compositions being in Castilian.

Corresponding exactly to the ballad section of Part I is the sixth group of Part II, which bears the rubric: "Here begin the ballads worth hearing about Roman deeds. Along with that of Leander and Hero." Timoneda correctly suggests in his heading that the first two ballads dealing with Leander and Hero are not related to Rome. But neither are the seventh and eighth, which concern respectively the

Lydian Queen Artemisia and the Athenian Prince Hippomenes. Of the twelve ballads, the most striking, from the point of view of theme, is the fourth, which is entitled "Ballad of How a Woman Came to Be Pope in Rome." It deals with the mythical ninth-century female Pope Joan. Not surprisingly, this legend has attracted many writers,[13] including Boccaccio, *Concerning Famous Women*, Ch. 99, and Pedro Mexía, *Silva de varia lección* (1540, etc.), from whose Part I, Ch. 9, Timoneda probably derived his version. More recently, Lawrence Durrell, the author of the famous Alexandria Quartet, published the novel *Pope Joan*, a translation and adaptation from the Greek of Emmanuel Royidis (1835–1904). With the exception of this ballad on Pope Joan, all the *romances* of this section were reprinted in Timoneda's *Rosas de romances* of 1573. Romeu (pp. 69–70) makes a good case for Timoneda's being the author of these twelve ballads.

The penultimate section of Part II is described by Timoneda in the following rubric: "Here begin *villancicos* and *canciones* in the manner of a pastoral dialogue, on diverse amorous events." Once more the compiler turns to the popular genres that have been seen so often, but this time thirteen of the nineteen are structured as dialogues between conventionalized pastoral figures: Carillo and Zagala, Gil and Bras, etc. All the poems are in Castilian.

The eighth and last section comprises a traditional-sounding poem, composed of a refrain and a one-stanza gloss, in which a lover bemoans his lady's cruelty. This poem, in turn, is glossed in eleven strophes written in less popular style.

Those who have examined the *Flor de enamorados* (Flower of Lovers) most closely (Rodríguez-Moñino and Devoto, Romeu, Fuster) regard it as one of the most important collections of its kind and era, not only for its copiousness, careful organization, and the variety of its genres, styles, and sources, but also for the high quality of many of its lyrics.

## III Villete de amor

Timoneda's next datable anthology bears the title *Cancionero llamado Villete de amor, compuesto por Bautista Montidea* (Songbook Called Billet-doux of Love, Composed by Bautista Montidea). The latter surname is an obvious anagram of Timoneda while the Valencian's Christian name, Juan, is suggested by Bautista, the second half of the common baptismal name Juan Bautista. Printed in

Valencia around 1565 according to Salvá,[14] This brief octavo booklet consists of sixteen leaves divided into two *cuadernos*, or gatherings, each with its own title page as well as its own set of signatures. Each section is specifically dedicated to the court jester Luis Quirosillo, thus suggesting the entertaining nature of the contents.

The first *cuaderno* begins with nine examples of the now familiar *canción* (four-line refrain plus gloss) on amorous or amorous-pastoral themes. The last selection, entitled "Contienda de colores" (Debate of Colors), comprises nine octosyllabic octaves plus a *villancico* (three-line refrain plus gloss) which serves as a "deshecha," that is, as a conclusion or a sort of envoi.

The most interesting poem of the first *cuaderno* is this "Contienda de colores" (Debate of Colors), which weds the tradition of the medieval debate to that of the defense of the *morena*. After the Judge has declared Dark to be superior to Red and Green, the poet concludes by glossing the following popular refrain:

| | |
|---|---|
| No desprecies, morenica,<br>[la] tu color tan morena,<br>que esa es la color buena.<br>(fol. [a viii] verso) | Don't despise, dear swarthy girl,<br>your color so brown,<br>for that is the good color. |

The second *cuaderno* bears the new subtitle *Enfados de muy grandes avisos, y provechosas sentencias, nunca impresos, ni vistos hasta agora. Puestos a gesto por Montidea, grande amigo de Diamonte* (Annoyances of Very Great Counsel, and Beneficial Adages, Never Before Printed nor Seen. Arranged by Montidea, Great Friend of Diamonte). The latter surname is, like the earlier one, an anagram of Timoneda. The title poem consists of forty-one eleven-syllable tercets plus a final four-line strophe, or *cuarteto*. In this work, each stanza of which begins with a form of the verb *enfadar* ("to annoy"), the author complains of numerous human follies: the faithless husband, the religious hypocrite, the author who belittles every other writer's work, etc., etc.

Also in terza rima is the next selection, headed "Tercetos de Montemayor." The poem, which begins "Pasaba Amor su arco desarmado," is taken from Montemayor's famed pastoral novel *La Diana* (1559?), Book III. In sharp contrast to the preceding lament, in which Belisa cries out against Love and Fortune, are the next two poems. These deal with the notorious Diego Moreno, the traditional figure of the cuckold, a comic subject that appears not only in

Timoneda's poetry but also in his theater and prose fiction. In the first, Diego has unexpectedly turned jealous; in the second, his wife expresses her annoyance at this change in her previously complacent husband. Both poems were reprinted by Timoneda in his *El truhanesco* (The Comic One, 1573), the second one in truncated form. The brief anthology concludes with a pastoral *canción* on the *carpe diem* theme. It is not without some irony that, after revealing the mutual recriminations of Diego Moreno and his wife, the poet tells the pretty young shepherdess of this last poem to enjoy her "tender years."

## IV *The* Cancioneros *of 1573*

The year 1573 saw the publication by Timoneda of four more brief *cancioneros* (songbooks), this time in duodecimo and twelve leaves in length: *Enredo de amor, Guisadillo de amor, El truhanesco,* and *Dechado de colores.* The Austrian National Library (Vienna) owns the unique extant copies of the original editions but, in 1951, Rodríguez-Moñino reprinted in a single volume the first three and part of the fourth.

The *Enredo de amor* (Tangle of Love) consists of twelve *canciones* and four *villancicos* of the usual amorous and amorous-pastoral types. The third poem stands out for its effective, though limited, use of *sayagués,* the conventional pastoral dialect so widely employed by poets and playwrights of the Golden Age. This amusing *canción,* in which a shepherdess protests her innocence of any disloyalty toward her shepherd, begins with the following refrain:

| | |
|---|---|
| Querelloso está Pascual<br>porque yo a Lorente abré;<br>si lo hiz, descuido hue,<br>no lo quillotré por mal.<br>(fol. 2 verso) | Pascual is complaining<br>because I spoke to Llorente;<br>if I did it, it was a slip,<br>I didn't attract him for evil's sake. |

The title page of the *Enredo* states that this *cancionero* is "agora nuevamente compuesto" ("now newly composed") by Timoneda. Although the Valencian bookseller at times used "composed" in its meaning of "adapted" or "gathered together," it seems likely that some of these compositions are indeed his. Three successive *canciones* ("¿Por qué olvidas el rebaño?"; "Aquel si viene o no viene"; "Pastora, que en el cayado") appear also in broadsides of one sheet published by Timoneda.

The title page of the second songbook reads: *Cancionero llamado Guisadillo de amor. Agora nuevamente compuesto y guisado por Joan Timoneda de diversos autores, para los enfermos y disgustados amadores; en el cual se contienen canciones y extrañísimas glosas* (Songbook Entitled Potpourri of Love. Now Newly Composed and Prepared by Juan Timoneda from Different Authors, for Sick and Disgusted Lovers; in Which Are Contained *Canciones* and Very Fine *Glosas.)* On the back of this folio, the compiler describes the poems as "las mejores que jamás se hayan visto" ("the best that have ever been seen").

Following seven of the familiar *canciones* on amorous and amorous-pastoral themes are eleven *glosas* of three types that have not been seen before in Timoneda's anthologies. Needless to say, all three types deal with love, but each has a different metrical scheme, consisting of a refrain and its gloss. In the first type, the refrain, called *canción,* consists of four verses, each of which, in successive order, forms the last line of the four stanzas of the gloss. Similarly, in the second type, the refrain, called *villancico,* consists of three verses, each of which, in successive order, forms the last line of the three stanzas of the gloss. Finally, in the third type, the refrain, called *mote,* consists of a single verse which then forms the last line of the single-strophed gloss.

Two of the *Guisadillo*'s poems appear in whole or in part also in broadsides published by Timoneda: the refrain of "Cuando Menga quiere a Bras"; both the refrain and the gloss of "Zagala, tente a la rama." The first of these *canciones* concerns the shepherd Bras, who rejects the love of the shepherdess Menga for her having earlier rejected him; in the second, a departing shepherd promises to be faithful to his beloved, while urging her to be true to him. Moreover, the first five verses ("Afuera, consejos vanos," etc.) of the gloss of "Quitaos allá, desengaños" appear as a song in Cervantes' play *El rufián dichoso,* Act I.

In an apparent effort to provide an amatory song or poem for every occasion, Timoneda assembled a *cancionero* entitled *El truhanesco compilado por Joan Timoneda, en el cual se contienen apacibles y graciosas canciones para cantar. Con todas las obras del honrado Diego Moreno, que hasta aquí se han compuesto* (The Comic One Compiled by John Timoneda, in Which Are Contained Pleasant and Comic Songs to Be Sung. With All the Works about the Honorable Diego Moreno That Have Been Composed to Date). In the first of these ten *canciones,* the poet ridicules prostitutes who try to pass as ladies by taking the title "doña." Next, a thoroughly Hispanic song in which a man cries out "muera yo en cuernos de un toro / y no puestos por mujer" ("may I die on the horns of a bull / and not on those placed by a woman") precedes four *canciones* dealing specifically with the traditional cuckold Diego Moreno. As has been noted above on pp. 115–16, two of these Diego Moreno poems appeared earlier in the *Villete de amor* (Billet-doux of Love). In the seventh poem, "Marido tan bien mandado," a wife speaks with pleasure and scorn of her henpecked, cuckolded husband.

Despite its modern sound, the eighth poem deals with a traditional theme, the daughter who exclaims, "Si mi padre no me casa / yo seré escándalo de su casa." ("If my father doesn't allow me to marry / I'll be the scandal of his house"). The ninth poem, "Entrá en casa, Gil García," is a sort of sixteenth-century version of Maggie and Jiggs: poor Gil García can only beg his shrewish wife: "soltá el palo, mujer mía" ("put down the stick, my dear"). The popularity of this humorous composition shows in its appearance as part of a broadside published by Timoneda. As his final selection, the compiler includes a poem that repeats another ancient concept: even in matters of the heart, it's money that talks.

Although the title page of the fourth *cancionero, Dechado de colores* (Color Sampler), is missing from the earliest copy, the songbook is generally assumed to have been compiled by Timoneda and to have been printed by Juan Navarro in 1573, like the three other, typographically similar, *cancioneros* with which it is bound in the unique Vienna volume. As the title poem of the collection was reprinted, albeit in somewhat different form, in other places, it is not included in the edition here described.

The title poem, a series of fifteen *villancicos,* is based on the concept that each color worn by the poet's beloved possesses a symbolic meaning. Accordingly, in each poem the lover speaks to his lady in the context of the situation, emotion, or trait denoted by the color, interpreting or applying the symbolism in a personal—and sometimes surprising—way. In the second *villancico,* for instance, the poet states that, although yellow suggests despair, it is not true as far as he is concerned; he will not stop loving her. In number five, the poet does not see his lady's chastity as a virtue, but rather as cruelty toward him.

Following the title poem is a "Romance de amores, agora nuevamente compuesto, sobre aquel sujeto que está en la 'Fortuna de amor,' do se queja la lengua de los ojos, y los ojos del corazón, con delicadas sentencias que les da Cupido" (Ballad about Love, Now Newly Composed, on That Subject That Is in the "Fortuna de amor," Where the Tongue Complains about the Eyes, and the Eyes about the Heart, with Delicate Sentences That Cupid Gives Them) plus a "Canción por deshecha," or envoi, that begins "Entiendan los amadores" ("Let lovers understand"). The allusion in the ballad's title refers to the "Proceso de amor . . ." in Book II of Antonio de Lo Frasso's *Los diez libros de fortuna d'amor* (Barcelona: Pedro Malo, 1573; copy at The Hispanic Society), folios [62] recto to 70 verso. As the colophon of Lo Frasso's book is dated March 1, 1573, clearly Timoneda's work could not have been printed sooner than late 1573. Three biting glosses of the *mote* "Donde las toman las dan" center on the importance of money in matters of love. The final selection is an amorous *canción* that begins with the well-known refrain "Un abrazo me dio Inés."

## V Rosas de romances

The same year, 1573, that saw the publication of the four *cancioneros* described above also witnessed the appearance of Timoneda's four duodecimo *romanceros* (ballad collections): *Rosa de amores, Rosa española, Rosa gentil,* and *Rosa real.* In 1963, A. Rodríguez-Moñino and D. Devoto reprinted, under the collective title *Rosas de romances* (Roses of Balladry), all four of the unique original copies owned by the Austrian National Library.

Unlike the anthologies described thus far, which contain a variety of metrical forms, these four comprise almost exclusively a single form: the *romance,* or ballad. The *romance,* the Spanish meter par excellence, is defined by Mrs. del Río as "a brief epico-lyric poem of an indefinite number of octosyllabic verses, the even ones rhyming assonantally, which was sung or recited to the sound of a musical instrument in order to entertain an audience or for dancing. It was sung, and is still sung, without musical accompaniment, for individual solace by men and women in their daily tasks, or in family gatherings."[15]

Timoneda, as he explains in the Preface of the *Rosa de amores*, having accumulated a large number of ballads—some his own compositions; others, old, anonymous ones—divided them into four parts or categories for presentation to the public. He does not, however, identify which poems are his, nor does he indicate the sources of the others.

The "old" ones derive from oral tradition or from such earlier collections as the *Cancionero de romances* (Antwerp, 1547–1548, etc.) and the *Silva de varios romances* (Zaragoza, 1550, etc.). Many of his own ballad compositions had appeared earlier in the *Flor de enamorados,* as we have seen.

Part I, the *Rosa de amores* (Garland of Love), is some seventy-two leaves in length and contains fifty-five ballads. Though restricted in meter and theme, the collection offers a wide variety of subject matter. There are love stories from classical mythology (Hero and Leander, Procne and Philomela) and from classical legend (Alexander and Centilla, Antony and Cleopatra). Other lovers are Moorish (Abindarráez and Jarifa), pastoral (Sireno and Diana), chivalric (Amadís and Oriana), and even picaresque ("De Toledo sale el jaque").

Interesting from the point of view of literary history is the first poem of this part. A parody of the Cid ballad "Cabalga Diego Laínez," it enumerates many poets who have written of love; among them are Romans, fifteenth-century Spaniards, and sixteenth-century Valencians, including Timoneda himself. The poet describes himself with perhaps justified modesty as a "comarcano de poesía" ("near-poet"). Among the oldest anonymous ballads of this part are "Al pie de una verde haya" and "Bodas se hacen en Francia"; in the former, the Moorish King Galván describes his love for the Christian captive Moriana; in the latter, the poet relates the delicious, albeit unexemplary, episode that follows:

Bodas se hacen en Francia,
allá dentro de París.
¡Cuán bien que guía la danza
esa tal doña Beatriz!
Mas también se la miraba
ese Conde don Martín.
"¿Qué miráis aquí, buen conde?
Conde, ¿qué miráis aquí?
Decid si miráis la danza,
o si mirades a mí."
"Que no miro yo la danza,
porque muchas danzas vi;
miro yo vuestra lindeza

que ver no la merecí,
la cual me mata de amores,
y a ser vuestro me rendí."
"Si bien os parezco, Conde,
Conde, saquéisme de de aquí quí;
que el marido tengo viejo
y no nos podrá seguir."
*(Rosa de amores*, fol. 67 verso)

There is a wedding in France,
within the city of Paris.
How well she leads the dance
that famous Doña Beatriz!
But also watching her was
the well-known Count Don Martin.
"What are you watching, good Count?
Count, what are you looking at?
Tell me whether you're looking at the dance
or whether you're looking at me."
"I'm not watching the dance
because I've seen many of them;
I'm looking at your beauty
which I'm not worthy to see;
it fills me with love for you
and I'm now completely yours."
"If I look good to you, Count,
Count, take me away from here,
for my husband is quite old
and won't be able to pursue us."

Part II, *Rosa española* (Spanish Garland) deals with "historias de España" ("Spanish historical matters"), as the title page indicates. It is therefore Timoneda's first poetic collection whose predominant theme is not love. As in the case of Part I, Timoneda in the Preface to Part II states that this collection includes not only his own compositions, some written in his youth, others more recently, but also the work of others.

Some ninety-seven leaves in length, Part II contains sixty-eight *romances*. After an initial ballad on the miraculous rescue of a Catalan knight from the Moors, Timoneda once more exhibits his organizing ability by arranging the poems in groups dealing with the great epic subjects: Bernardo del Carpio, the Seven Infantes de Lara, the Siege of Zamora, the Cid, and Roderick, the Last Gothic King. These "historical" ballads, among the most famous in Spanish literature, are followed by fifteen "frontier" ballads, which deal with "cosas de Granada," according to Timoneda's heading—that is, the relations between Christian and Moor during the Reconquest of Granada.

A final group is made up of thirteen ballads that deal mainly with "historical" events in the other Peninsular kingdoms of Aragon and Portugal. Among the famous protagonists are Doña Isabel de Liar; Don Ramiro de Aragón, "El Monje"; and Don Pedro el Cruel.

Of the four parts, the *Rosa española* is the outstanding anthology, containing such classics as "Helo, helo, por do viene" (a Cid ballad), "Los vientos eran contrarios" (on Roderick, the Last Gothic King), "Abenámar, Abenámar," (a frontier ballad), and "Doña María de Padilla" (on King Pedro el Cruel), to mention only a few.

Part III bears the title *Rosa gentil* (Pagan Garland) and deals with "historias romanas y troyanas" ("Roman and Trojan histories"), according to the title page, which, in this respect, is not entirely accurate. The title *Rosa gentil* must have sounded out of place in post-Tridentine Spain, for Timoneda, in his Preface, urges the reader as follows: "Huele en ella el fundamento, y virtud por que aquellos gentiles osaban poner en riesgo sus personas y perder las vidas. Y a lo no tal dale de mano." ("In it [the garland] sniff the reason and virtue for which those pagans dared to risk their persons and to lose their lives. And pay no attention to the rest.")

Some seventy-two leaves in length, this collection comprises forty-nine ballads. Of these, nineteen had appeared earlier in Timoneda's *Sarao de amor*, in his *Flor de enamorados*, or in both. "Pagan" themes not previously treated include: the heroism of Numancia (Soria); Nero's burning of Rome; Androcles (Andronicus) and the lion; the abduction of Helen and the Trojan War; and the remarkable story of the peasant of the Danube that begins "A formar quejas a Roma." Having apparently exhausted his supply of "pagan" *romances*, Timoneda turns in the final dozen to more recent times.

Of particular interest to Valencians is the ballad "A veinte y siete de julio," for it deals with the murder in 1492 of one of the sons of the Valencian-born Pope Alexander VI. In this same final group of the *Rosa gentil* is found perhaps the most absurd and at the same time most fascinating of all the ballads published by Timoneda:

"Romance de una mujer que parió trescientos y setenta hijos" (Ballad of a Woman Who Gave Birth to Three Hundred and Seventy Babies). When Princess Margaret accuses a beggar woman of adultery, the latter curses her, with the result that the Princess gives birth to 370 mouse-sized babies. The Spanish original may be conveniently read in Durán's *Romancero general,* II *(Biblioteca de autores españoles,* Vol. 16), no. 1346. An English translation appears in W. S. Merwin's *Some Spanish Ballads* (London and New York: Abelard-Schuman, 1961), pp. 123–24.

The vitality of this story in oral and written forms is as astonishing as the tale itself. It clearly embodies beliefs that are still current in Spanish folklore, for J. M. Gómez-Tabanera, in discussing modern Spanish folk attitudes toward multiple births, reports that "sometimes it is thought that the multiple birth occurs as a punishment from heaven to avenge a grave offense to the honor of a woman whom the parturient has slandered as an adulteress for giving birth to twins."[16] As a folktale, the story also appears in Stith Thompson's *Motif-Index of Folk-Literature,* where several important studies of the theme are listed (Vol. V, p. 24: L435.2.1). In addition, the story is recorded by two physicians, George M. Gould, M.D., and Walter L. Pyle, M.D., in their *Anomalies and Curiosities of Medicine* . . . (Phila.: W. B. Saunders, 1896; reprint, N.Y.: Bell, 1956, p. 147).

Timoneda seems to have derived his version from the enormously popular *Jardín de flores curiosas* (Salamanca: Juan Bautista de Terranova, 1570) by Antonio de Torquemada.

In the first *tratado* of his work, Torquemada includes all the basic elements that are found in Timoneda: (1) the protagonist is Princess or Countess Margarita of Ireland, (2) she is cursed by a beggar woman whom she has accused of adultery, (3) as a result of the curse, Margarita gives birth to 366 (not 370) babies, (4) the babies, the size of small mice, are baptized by a bishop, (5) the baptismal vessel was touched by Emperor Charles V, and (6) the truth of the story is attested to by Enrico Buceburgense, Baptista Fulgoso, and Luis Vives. Timoneda's other authority, "Algozar," is not cited here by Torquemada but the latter does mention "Algazar, an ancient philosopher of very great authority" in a later passage of the same *tratado.*

Perhaps the ultimate irony of this tale of multiple birth is the fact that St. Margaret is the patroness of pregnant women!

The fourth and final *romancero,* entitled *Rosa real* (Royal Garland), is some eighty-four folios in length and contains twenty-two ballads as well as five *villancicos* and two *canciones*. In the words of the title page, the *Rosa real* deals with "casos señalados de reyes y otras personas que han tenido cargos importantes, así como príncipes, visorreyes y arzobispos" ("notable events about kings and other persons who have held important offices, such as princes, viceroys, and archbishops"). In general, the ballads are versified news reports on sixteenth-century events, usually showing the date of the happening, and, in some cases, accompanied by a personal commentary in the form of a *villancico* or a *canción*. The events described range chronologically from the capture of King Francis I of France at the battle of Pavia on February 24, 1525 (not 1530 as indicated in the *romancero),* to the Massacre of St. Bartholomew in August, 1572. A majority of the poems concern incidents that occurred between 1550 and 1572. It is likely that Timoneda himself wrote most of these.

Some of the themes are national or international in scope, for example, the Sack of Rome (1527), the coronation of Charles V (1530), his death (1558), and the Battle of Lepanto (1571). Other topics, however, are specifically Valencian: the death of the Viceroy of Valencia, Fernando de Aragón (1550); the death of the Archbishop of Valencia, Tomás de Villanueva (1555); the appointment of Francisco de Navarra as new Archbishop of Valencia (1556).

Though the prosaic ballads of this anthology lack the poetic qualities of the historical ballads on epic subjects seen in the *Rosa española,* many were nevertheless very popular in the Golden Age. Sixteen of them were reprinted, anonymously, in the *Flor de romances* . . . (Zaragoza: Juan Soler, 1578). Furthermore, the ballad "Triste estaba el Padre Santo," which deals with the Sack of Rome, appeared in thirty-nine other collections of the sixteenth and seventeenth centuries.

Timoneda's contribution to Hispanic balladry may be summed up in the words of C. C. Smith: ". . . he was but an indifferent original composer, but posterity is much indebted to him as a collector of traditional ballads and variants, many of them known from no other source."[17]

## VI Pliegos sueltos

In addition to the relatively accessible collections that have been described in the preceding pages, Timoneda also published many poems in now rare *pliegos sueltos* (chapbooks). The *pliego suelto,* in the words of Rodríguez-Moñino, is, "in general, a quarternion [gathering] of few leaves destined to disseminate literary or historical texts among the great reading public, particularly the popular masses. Its extension varies according to that of the work that is contained and thus, although at first the norm was actually a *pliego,* that is, a sheet of paper in its natural size, folded twice to form eight pages, little by little the concept has been expanding and the gathering of up to thirty-two pages or even more is considered as a *pliego suelto.*"[18] Concerning the vitality of this genre, the great bibliographer states:

> And the most important thing is that many of these chapbooks, of very varied content, have been printed without interruption from the end of the fifteen century to our own days, without the reader's being concerned by the anachronistic character of the events narrated nor the decrepitude of worn-out poetic forms: let us consider only the fact that in the midst of the twentieth century, there continue to be reprinted the ballads of the Marqués de Mantua, those of the naval battle of Lepanto, the *Pasión trovada* of Diego de San Pedro and the old *quintillas* about the *Renegada de Valladolid.*[19]

To give the reader an idea of Timoneda's poetic chapbook production, I shall describe only those reprinted by Gallardo and by Lucas de Torre. Of the two *pliegos sueltos* reprinted by Gallardo,[20] the first bears the title *Diversas y nuevas canciones muy sentidas para cantar. Compuestas por Juan Timoneda* (Different and New Songs, Very Eloquent for Singing. Composed by Juan Timoneda). This single sheet in cuarto comprises the three *canciones* that begin "Aquel si viene o no viene," "Cuando Menga quiere a Bras," and "¿Por qué olvidas el rebaño?" As already noted, the first and third poems also appear in Timoneda's *Enredo de amor* (Tangle of Love), while the refrain of the second appears with a different gloss in the *Guisadillo de amor* (Potpourri of Love). The other chapbook reprinted by Gallardo is entitled *Coplas del honradísimo Gil García. Compuestas por Juan Timoneda* (The Songs of the Very Honorable Gil García. Composed by Juan Timoneda). This single sheet in cuarto includes not only the title poem but also the *canciones* that begin "Zagala, tente a la rama" and "Pastora que en el cayado." All three poems appear in other collections of Timoneda's: the first, in

*El truhanesco* (The Comic One); the second, in *Guisadillo de amor;* the third, in *Enredo de amor.*

Under the title "Varias poesías de Juan Timoneda," Lucas de Torre reprinted twelve of the Valencian's *pliegos sueltos* in the *Boletín de la Real Academia Española.*[21] Of the twenty poems included in these chapbooks, all but eight are either devotional or the secular originals of spiritual *contrafacta.* Since religious themes have not been discussed previously in this chapter, it will be appropriate to devote some attention to them here, while merely enumerating the nonreligious poems. The latter include four comic dialogues, a love sonnet, two amorous-pastoral *canciones,* and a new version of the popular Catalan song "Bella de vós só enamorós" (see Chapter 8).

Of the devotional poems all but two are spiritual *contrafacta,* or, as they are called in Spanish, *versiones a lo divino,* that is, divinizations of secular poetry, wherein the poet rewrites a secular poem by giving it a spiritual meaning. In the octaves "María para Adán, dulce y sabrosa" and the sonnet "Criando el mundo Dios el animoso," Timoneda divinizes respectively the poems "Flérida para mí, dulce y sabrosa" and "Pasando el mar Leandro el animoso" by Garcilaso de la Vega, the texts of which are included in the chapbook. Another poem bears the title "Danza espiritual de muchas mujeres señaladas de la Sagrada Escritura. Hecha en alabanza de la Sacratísima Madre de Dios. Tañida por Juan Timoneda. Ahora nuevamente en el año 1553" (Spiritual Dance of Many Notable Women of Holy Scripture. Done in Praise of the Most Holy Mother of God. Performed by Juan Timoneda. Now Recently in the Year 1553). In this case, Timoneda utilizes the words of a popular song, "Pase la galana, pase / pase la galana" ("Let the lady pass by, let her pass / let the lady pass by"), to demonstrate that the Virgin Mary superseded all the great ladies of the Old Testament.

Three poems, two in Spanish and one in Catalan, are spiritual *contrafacta* for Christmas; they begin: "Un chiste muy de notar,/ / señores, contaré yo," "Yo sé a quién / de amores le fue muy bien," and "Da-li Miquel / porta'm a casa." The poem "El que sin ti vivir / ya no querría" is, as Timoneda himself explains, a divinization, in praise of the Immaculate Conception, of the epistle by Boscán that begins with the same words. Finally, there is another poem with the significant title "La gallarda contrahecha a lo espiritual por Juan Timoneda en alabanza de Nuestro Redentor Jesucristo" (The Galliard [a dance] Divinized by Juan Timoneda in Praise of Our Redeemer Jesus Christ).

Of the two poems that are not *versiones a lo divino,* one is a prayer directed to Timoneda's fellow Valencian, St. Vincent Ferrer (died 1419). The other is, in this writer's opinion, the most impressive of Timoneda's religious poems. A *romance* written in octosyllabic couplets in consonance, the poem bears the title "Romance de la Sacratísima Pasión de Nuestro Redentor Jesucristo . . ." (Ballad of the Most Sacred Passion of Our Redeemer Jesus Christ . . .). Beginning with the verse "Llorad, devotos cristianos" ("Weep, devout Christians"), it proceeds for a total of 234 lines, fully half of them starting with the hypnotic "llorad" ("weep"), which is repeated like the tolling of a funeral bell. This anaphora brings to mind not only the reiterated "ora pro nobis" of religious litanies, but also the highly effective use of repetition in St. John of the Cross's "Cantar del alma que se huelga de conocer a Dios por fe" ("aunque es de noche") and in García Lorca's "Llanto por Ignacio Sánchez Mejías" ("a las cinco de la tarde"). Strikingly similar is the use of the verb "weep" as the initial word in eleven of the twelve stanzas of the Hebrew poem "Lament on the Devastation of the Land of Israel (1012)" by Joseph Ibn Abithur, who was born in the middle of the tenth century in the southwestern Spanish city of Mérida (see David Goldstein, translator, *The Jewish Poets of Spain 900–1250,* Penguin Books, revised and enlarged edition, 1971, pp. 39–40).

So much poetic activity requires an overall assessment. To Timoneda the anthologist, Spanish literature will ever be indebted for his having preserved so many worthy poems, particularly those of a traditional or popular character. His stature as a poet, however, cannot be adequately evaluated as long as the authorship of such a large number of the poems he published remains unknown. Nonetheless, on the assumption that many lyrics are indeed his, the Valencian has won for himself an honorable place among Spanish Golden Age poets, as will be demonstrated in Chapter 9.

CHAPTER 6

# *Timoneda as Editor of Named Authors*

AS we have seen, Timoneda frequently adapted or edited the work of unidentified writers in his poetic anthologies and other collections. In this chapter, I shall treat the several cases wherein he edited the work of other authors whom he specifically names. As was already noted, the Valencian bookseller, in the judgment of Cervantes, earned eternal fame for having edited the works of Lope de Rueda.

## I *Juan Aragonés*

Timoneda's earliest editorial work of this type appears in 1563 in the Medina del Campo edition of the *Sobremesa y alivio de caminantes* (and again in the edition of Alcalá, 1576). Preceding his own stories, the Valencian publishes twelve others "of another author named Juan Aragonés—may he rest in peace." Absolutely nothing more is known about Juan Aragonés. Menéndez y Pelayo laments the small number of his tales "because they have a more national character than those of Timoneda" (p. 73). As examples of this "national character," the great polygraph cites the two (nos. 2 and 12) that involve the famous poet Garci Sánchez de Badajoz as well as the three (nos. 7, 8, 11) that refer to the court jester Velasquillo. Because he was unable to examine Timoneda's *Buen aviso* (1564), Don Marcelino was not aware that the Valencian would publish in that collection variants of four of Juan Aragonés' tales: no. 5 (see *Buen aviso,* I, 36); no. 9 (see *Buen aviso,* I, 18); no. 10 (*Buen aviso,* II, 68); no. 11 (*Buen aviso,* II, 89).

## II *Alonso de la Vega*

Timoneda's next edition of a named author bears the title *Las tres famosísimas comedias del ilustre poeta y gracioso representante Alonso de la Vega* (The Three Very Famous Plays of the Illustrious

Author and Comic Actor Alonso de la Vega) (Valencia: Juan Navarro [?], 1566). Aside from the fact that Alonso de la Vega was a resident of Seville in 1560 and that he acted in that city's Corpus Christi performances of the same year, nothing is known about this man except what can be gleaned from the front matter of Timoneda's edition. These gleanings are that, after spending some time at the court, the author-actor went to Valencia, where he wrote these three plays and where he died. All three, *Comedia Tolomea* (The Comedy of the Ptolomies), *Tragedia Serafina* (The Tragedy of Serafina), and *Comedia de la Duquesa de la Rosa* (The Comedy of the Duchess de la Rosa), are written in prose and are far from being first-rate but, as we have seen in Chapter 3, the first and third are related to *patraña* I and *patraña* VII, respectively.

It should be recalled that Timoneda made no attempt to hide the connection between the two Italianate plays and his two *patrañas*. Nor can we fail to appreciate his disarming candor in stating his reason for publishing Alonso de la Vega's plays: in the "Epistle to the Pious Reader" he points out that as a bookseller he seeks, "without harm to anyone, the wherewithal to make a profit."

Of the three plays, that of the *Duchess de la Rosa* is regarded as the best, Menéndez y Pelayo considering it superior to both Bandello's and Timoneda's versions of the same story (p. 84).

## III *Juan de Vergara*

In the following year, 1567, Timoneda, presumably for the same profit motive, published *Dos coloquios pastorales* (Two Pastoral Colloquies) (Valencia: Juan Mey) by Juan de Vergara. About Vergara little is known except that, in addition to being an author, he was also an actor and theatrical manager. Unfortunately, the two plays cannot be found today, but the book's existence was recorded by the seventeenth-century bibliographer Nicolás Antonio *(Bibliotheca hispana,* 1672, I, 607b–608a). Though Antonio makes no mention of Timoneda, investigators like Cotarelo[1] and Juliá Martínez,[2] among others, state that the Valencian published the plays. They base this assertion, I assume, on the fact that the Inventory of Timoneda's bookshop includes among unbound copies of books written or edited by the bookseller the following entry: "Item, 199 pastoral colloquies called *The Three Pastoral Colloquies,* two by Vergara and the other by Lope [de Rueda]."[3]

## IV *Lope de Rueda*

The year 1567 was an especially busy one for Timoneda; during its course appeared not only his edition of Vergara's plays and his own *Patrañuelo*, but also his first publication of plays by Lope de Rueda. At the famous printing house of Juan Mey, the bookseller published *Cuatro comedias y dos coloquios pastoriles del excelente poeta y gracioso representante Lope de Rueda* (Four Plays and Two Pastoral Colloquies of the Excellent Author and Comic Actor Lope de Rueda), a collection that includes the plays *Eufemia, Armelina, Los engañados* (The Deceived), *Medora*, and the colloquies *Camilla* and *Tymbria*. The same printing house that year brought out at the bookseller's expense the *Compendio llamado El Deleitoso, en el cual se contienen muchos pasos graciosos del excelente poeta y gracioso representante Lope de Rueda, para poner en principios y entremedias de coloquios y comedias. Recopilados por Juan Timoneda* (Compendium Called the Delightful One, in Which Are Contained Many Comic *Pasos* of the Excellent Author and Comic Actor Lope de Rueda to Place at the Beginning and in the Middle of Colloquies and Plays. Compiled by Juan Timoneda). The anthology comprises seven *pasos*, including the famous *Cornudo y contento* (Cuckolded and Content) and *Las aceitunas* (The Olives). Three years later, Timoneda published another collection of Rueda's works: *El registro de representantes* (The Register of Actors), "in which are included by Juan Timoneda many and comic *pasos* of Lope de Rueda, and other different authors, not only about lackeys and simpletons but also other diverse persons." This edition includes only three *pasos* that bear Rueda's name (the fourth, fifth, and sixth); the first three *pasos* and the *Coloquio llamado Prendas de amor* (Colloquy Called Tokens of Love) are anonymous.

In the case of Rueda, Timoneda comments more fully, though tantalizingly incompletely, on the nature of his editorial work. In the "Exculpatory Epistle of Juan Timoneda to the Prudent Reader" (1567) which precedes the plays *Eufemia* and *Armelina*, the Valencian says:

> Beloved reader, when the plays of the excellent author and comic actor Lope de Rueda came into my hands, I recalled the desire and wish that some friends and lords of mine had to see them in useful and artful print. Therefore I arranged (with all possible care) to put them in order and to submit them to the correction of Holy Mother Church. For this reason,

from them have been removed some illicit and offensive things that some [spectators] have probably heard during Lope's lifetime. Consequently, remember that I'm not to blame, for my good intention is what saves me.

Equally interesting is the "Epistle of Juan Timoneda to the Esteemed Reader" (1567) that precedes the plays *Los engañados* (The Deceived) and *Medora:*

Most wise reader: the work that I have had in bringing out and having printed the present plays of the excellent author and comic actor Lope de Rueda, don't think that it has been a single one, [for it has been] very many and of considerable amount. The first was to write each one of them twice, and while writing them (as their author didn't intend to have them printed), because I found repeated some blunderings, or rather jokes, in the mouths of simpletons, negresses or lackeys, I was obliged to remove what was said twice in some of them and add others in their place. Then, [I was obliged] to go and have them read by the theologian who was assigned so that he could correct them and they could be printed. And finally, [there is] the deposit of my poor purse. Well, as one who performed so many labors to give you some honest and pleasant entertainment, I beg you that another not be added by your hand by your wishing to reproach me for my daily and proper activity, for I was born to serve you and to spend my life in this poor ability that God gave me.

In view of these statements, one must ask, what is the extent of the Valencian's intervention in the writings of the Sevillan goldbeater? De Chasca says: "It is to be regretted that Timoneda did not interest himself in the publication of his friend Rueda's works before the latter's death, and especially before 1559, when the first printed *Index* [*librorum prohibitorum*] was published. Before this date the many *gracias* [jokes], *descuydos* [blunderings] and *cosas no licitas* [illicit things] which were deleted by Timoneda and the *theologo* [theologian] would have remained to enliven even more the dialogue of the goldbeater's *simples, negras, pajes* and *lacayos* [simpletons, negresses, pages, and lackeys]."[4] The fact is, however, that we have no evidence that "many" passages were deleted nor do we know that the theologian removed any. Juliá Martínez[5] expresses the opposite opinion: "The corrections which [Timoneda] allowed himself to introduce into the text must not have been of great consequence, given the respect that the Valencian always showed toward Rueda." More realistic is the view of Crawford (p. 114): "We are unable to determine whether Timoneda limited himself to changes of minor importance or whether he actually attempted to rewrite the plays."

More recently F. González Ollé has taken up on three occasions the subject of Timoneda's intervention in Rueda's plays.[6] Unfortunately, though, his most detailed study of the topic is not yet accessible and I must rely on his preliminary assessments. First of all, the Spanish investigator insists—correctly, I believe—that Timoneda must be credited with establishing the definitive text of Rueda's plays. Second, according to González, Timoneda is responsible for the presence of a considerable number of Valencianisms (or Catalanisms) in the plays, a hypothesis that, in my opinion, is more difficult to prove in view of the fact that Rueda is known to have resided in the city on the Turia (see Chapter 2, p. 17 and its n. 4).

## V *Pedro Hurtado*

In 1569 Timoneda edited with a prologue a songbook *(cancionero)* composed by a certain Pedro Hurtado. The full title is *Cancionero llamado Recreo de amadores, en el cual se contienen canciones, villancicos, sonetos y excelentes octavas y otras obras y ahora nuevamente compuesto por Pedro Hurtado* (Songbook Called Recreation of Lovers, in Which Are Contained *Canciones, Villancicos,* Sonnets, and Excellent Octaves and Other Works, and Now Newly Composed by Pedro Hurtado). What little is known about this no longer extant volume is included in Rodríguez-Moñino's *Manual bibliográfico,* I, 530–531.

## CHAPTER 7

# *Nonfiction*

IN this chapter several of Timoneda's very rare nonfictional works will be described briefly. Of relatively minor importance, these works nevertheless exemplify popular publishing activities of the sixteenth century.

### I Cartilla de la muerte

Chronologically first among these publications is the *Cartilla de la muerte* (Primer of Death; Valencia: Joan Navarro, 1568). That the work belongs to the well-known genre called *ars moriendi* is clear from the subtitle, which reads: "Art to aid in dying well; in which is contained what can be said to a good Christian at the hour of death." This short work of some thirty-two leaves is recorded by the bibliographers Fuster, Martí Grajales, and Palau[1] and there is said to be a copy at the Library of the University of Valencia.

### II *The Three* Memorias

Of greater interest are the three lists that Timoneda published under the titles *Memoria hispanea* (Hispanic Memorandum); *Memoria poética* (Poetic Memorandum); and *Memoria valentina* (Valencian Memorandum). I shall describe them as they appear at the end of the *Sobremesa y alivio de caminantes* (Valencia: Joan Navarro, 1569).

The *Memoria hispanea,* only eight folios in length, consists of seventy-one short paragraphs—each with its own heading—on some domestic or foreign event that, in Timoneda's view, had a noteworthy impact on the history of Spain or was otherwise memorable. The first entry describes the origins of Mohammedanism and thus serves as background for the second entry on the invasion of Spain by the Moors and their defeat of King Roderick. Not surprising in light of Timoneda's professional activities is the ninth entry, which reports that "in the year 1459 the art of printing was invented by a German in the city of Mainz." The last item records the death of Philip II's wife Isabel in 1568. Not all events are equally momentous, however. For example, Timoneda devotes his forty-seventh entry to the fact that in the year 1546 the feasts of Corpus Christi and of St. John the Baptist occurred on the same day. He adds that this would not happen again until the year 1642. One must recall that Corpus Christi and St. John's Eve (Midsummer's Night) were very great festivals in Spain and that the feast of St. John the Baptist (June 24) was the onomastic, or saint's day, of the author's son, Juan Bautista, and probably his own. In at least one case, we find some of the anecdotal flavor that characterizes the *Sobremesa* and the *Buen aviso*. The eighth entry is entitled "A Very Great Miracle" and is as follows:

"In the year 1454, a Jew's young son went to confession and received Holy Communion along with his Christian companions. When the boy's father found out, he hurled the boy into a lighted oven. But the boy came out unharmed, explaining that a Lady whom he had seen in the church, who held a Child in her arms, had extinguished the fire with her hand."

Thus Timoneda records *as history* a very famous Marian legend[2] that frequently has anti-Semitic overtones. The three best-known Peninsular versions of this tale are those of King Alphonse the Wise *(Songs of Saint Mary,* no. 4), Gonzalo de Berceo *(Miracles of Our Lady,* no. 16), and Clemente Sánchez de Vercial *(Book of Exempla by A, B, C,* no. 269 [200]). Timoneda's version differs from the three just named in two significant details: the boy goes to confession before receiving Communion and there is no mention of the father's being punished.

Other early editions of the *Memoria hispanea* are: Zaragoza: Miguel de Guesa, 1563; Alcalá de Henares: Sebastián Martínez, 1576; Amberes: Antonio Tylenio, 1577; Toledo: Juan Ruiz, 1593; Sevilla: Fernando de Lara, 1603.

The *Memoria poética* comprises only one folio, although the title is on part of the previous folio. Using "poet" in its broad etymological sense of "author," Timoneda lists twenty-three writers along with the year in which they "flourished." He begins with eleven Latin authors from Seneca to Claudian. Following are three Italians: Dante, Petrarch, and the humanist Lorenzo Valla. Finally comes the Iberian group, which is especially curious: three are of Catalonian or Valencian origin (Jaume Roig, Boscán, Juan Fernández de Heredia); all the others (with the exception of Garcilaso de la Vega) are "New Christians" (Juan de Mena, Diego de San Pedro, Torres Naharro, Juan del Encina, Montemayor). Timoneda's chronology is, of course, not reliable; for example, Lorenzo Valla is said to have flourished in the year 1340 whereas in fact he was born in 1407 and died in 1457 (Avery, *The New Century Italian Renaissance Encyclopedia).* The only other edition of this work that has come to my attention is that of Zaragoza: Miguel de Guesa, 1563.

The *Memoria valentina,* ten folios in length, consists of seventy-nine individually titled short paragraphs on some event in the history of Valencia from its apocryphal founding "by Romo in the year 968 after the Flood of Noah" to the year 1569, which saw the installation of Juan de Ribera as Archbishop of Valencia. The Moorish impact on Valencian history is reflected in some eleven entries (events of 1087, 1229, 1238, 1455, 1503, 1525, 1526, 1538, 1550, 1562, and 1563). Again, the multiethnic character of Valencian society appears in the entry entitled "A Negro Who Sang Mass": "On 29 June 1552, the feast of St. Peter, Mass was sung in the [Dominican] convent of St. Catherine of Siena by a Negro. The Valencian-born black priest was the son of black slaves belonging to Matthew Ros."

The anecdote-like *format* of these entries is sometimes coupled with an anecdotal *content* that is quite in keeping with the highly condensed, elliptical tales of the *Sobremesa* and the *Buen aviso* (although, of course, the wit and humor are generally lacking), as in, for example, "The Dancer": "On 29 June 1532, the Vicar of the Archbishop of Valencia held up to public shame a Genoese man because he was constantly dancing. The man gave the following explanation: on a certain occasion he was dancing along the street with some companions when the Blessed Sacrament passed; they didn't kneel and by miracle were unable to stop dancing. For his misbehavior the Genoese was flogged in the streets of Valencia. Thereafter he danced no more." As in the case of the *Memoria poética,* bibliographers record only one other edition of the *Memoria valentina*: Zaragoza: Miguel de Guesa, 1563.

## III Timón de tratantes

In 1575, the ever pragmatic businessman Timoneda published an enlarged edition of a compilation of his called *Timón de tratantes* (Retailers' Guide) with the following description as part of the title:

"very necessary and useful to know by every retailer who may have to give or receive money, and pay salaries, and rentals, with other things that are very important for merchants." In short, it is a currency converter, consisting of five chapters, or tables. A description of the first one will suffice to give the reader an idea of the book in general. The table in question enables the user to convert Castilian *reales* into Valencian *libras, sueldos,* and *dineros* as well as into Castilian *maravedís* and Saragossan-Catalonian *libras*. The table covers from one *real* (at a value of twenty-three Castilian *dineros* each) to twenty thousand *reales*.

Finally it should be noted in connection with this work that its Spanish title, *Timón de tratantes (timón:* "rudder," literally), illustrates the widespread practice in the Golden Age of referring obliquely to an author's surname. This same association *timón* / Timoneda is found in the Valencian's *Betrothal of Christ ( Introito y argumento)* and in Melchor Horta's laudatory sonnet to Timoneda at the beginning of the *Ternario sacramental.*

## IV Libro llamado Ingenio

Like so many aspects of this author's life and work, the last nonfictional treatise to be discussed abounds in unsolved problems. In 1931, Francisco Vindel made known the existence of a posthumous publication previously unknown to Timoneda bibliographers: *Book Called Skill, Which Deals with the Game of Checkers, Done by Juan Timoneda. Dedicated to the Very Magnificent Gentleman, Don Iñigo de Losca, Captain in the Galleys of Spain. To Which Have Been Added Eight Plays of Great Skill, by Antonio Mirón y del Castillo.* In Tolosa. At the Establishment of Juan Bovde [Boude?], Ordinary Printer of His Majesty, 1635.[3] Vindel reproduces the title page and one other page. I have not succeeded in ascertaining the whereabouts of this book nor have I been able to further identify Iñigo de Losca and Mirón y del Castillo. Nor is anything known about a seventeenth-century printer named Bovde (or Boude) in Tolosa, a small town in the Basque province of Guipúzcoa. In fact, the existence of this book suggests the need to revise the history of printing in the province of Guipúzcoa. In his investigation of the latter subject, Fray Juan Ruiz de Larrinaga reports the temporary presence of a printer in the capital city of San Sebastián in 1584–1585 and the definitive establishment of printing in the province in 1667.[4] In the town of Tolosa, the earliest printer known to Fray Juan was Bernardo Ugarte (1696–1697).

Timoneda's treatise is of interest not only for the history of printing but also for that of checkers. It should be added to the five treatises on this game that the noted authority H. J. R. Murray lists as having appeared in Spain between 1547 and 1684. These works, in Murray's words, "point to a higher standard of play than was reached in any other country."[5] It is interesting to note that three of the treatises (those of Torquemada, Ruiz Montero, and Valls) were printed in Valencia.

CHAPTER 8

# *Works in Catalan-Valencian*

ALTHOUGH—as noted in the Biographical Sketch—Valencian was Timoneda's native tongue, only a small proportion of his works was written in that regional variety of the Catalan language. It is to the history of that language's literature, rather than to Castilian letters, that the works here considered belong. It must be pointed out also that only with some prior study can the average reader of Castilian understand colloquial Catalan-Valencian with any degree of ease. For these reasons the discussion will be brief. It will be convenient to treat these works under three headings: prose fiction, poetry, and theater.

## I *Prose Fiction*

Of the 161 anecdotes that comprise the *Sobremesa y alivio de caminantes* only two are written in Valencian: Part I, 6 and 75. The first purports to give the origin of the proverbial saying "Plore cascú son dol ab son cresol"[1] and is thus analogous to numbers 24–73 of Part II, which purport to explain the origin of proverbial sayings in Castilian. The second Valencian anecdote is based on a pun involving the Catalan word "cos" and is thus analogous to the many facetiae based on Castilian puns; for instance, numbers 15, 45, 46, 49, 58, and 63 in Part I of this same collection. As we have seen, 170 (complete) anecdotes comprise the *Buen aviso y portacuentos.* Of these, only one (I, 29) is entirely in Valencian; in another, (I, 61), the autobiographical tale cited on page 34, only the concluding verse is in Valencian.

## II *Poetry*

In Timoneda's earliest extant poetic anthology, *Sarao de amor* (1561), the index of Part II indicates that eight poems are in Valencian-Catalan but of these only five exist, four being *canciones* and one a *villancico.* The latter consists of a three-line refrain plus three octosyllabic stanzas, each of which repeats in its last verse the third line of the refrain. The traditional nature of this poem's theme is clearly revealed in the refrain: "If you have faith in women, / you'll be repaid with a thousand falsehoods: / beware, beware, don't trust them!" Part I includes a "Sonnet in Seven Languages," one of which is Valencian, as well as a "Sonnet on the Death of Our Emperor Charles Fifth, in Two Languages"—i.e., in Castilian and Valencian. All seven of the above-mentioned poems have been reprinted recently (1973) by Joan Fuster.[2]

Our author's second poetic anthology, *Flor de enamorados* (Flower of Lovers, 1562) comprises some 280 items according to the enumeration of Josep Romeu i Figueras.[3] Of these, fifty-four are in Catalan and one *canción* is bilingual, combining Castilian and Catalan. The fifty-four poems are almost equally divided between *canciones* (twenty-five) and *villancicos* (twenty-nine) and have also been reprinted recently by Joan Fuster. Among the best-known compositions is the *canción* "Bella, de vós só enamorós" which begins with the refrain: "Beautiful, I'm in love with you. / Would that you were mine! / Night and day, when I think of you, / my heart does sigh." This refrain is followed by five eight-line stanzas in which octosyllabic and pentasyllabic lines alternate. The seventh and eighth verses repeat the third and fourth lines of the refrain. Josep Romeu i Figueras, who has studied the diffusion of the popular tune that is here glossed, points out that Timoneda published three other versions of it: (1) a spiritual *contrafactum* in Castilian (at the end of his *Auto del Nacimiento),* (2) a spiritual *contrafactum* in Catalan (in a chapbook, or *pliego suelto),* and (3) another secular version in Catalan (in a chapbook reprinted by Joan Fuster). Also noted by the same Catalan scholar are four versions by other poets (Romeu, pp. 38–39).

In addition to the two chapbooks in Catalan that have just been mentioned, there are two others that require inclusion at this point: (1) a spiritual *contrafactum* for Christmas that begins "Les cobles de 'Da-li Miquel' " reprinted by Lucas de Torre and (2) the chapbook beginning "El Pater Noster glosado," which includes two Christmas songs in Catalan that have been reprinted by Joan Fuster. Finally, a love song in Catalan serves as a space-filler at the end of the *Farsa llamada Paliana* (1564) in the collection of plays called *Turiana.*

Before leaving the topic of Timoneda's poetry in Catalan, I would like to quote the opinion of a Valencian-speaker in this regard: "... the Catalan poems of the *Flower of Lovers* have a graceful dignity of diction: their language is vivid and flavorful. The pace of the verse shows a pleasant mathematical precision. And the color of the phrases, the impact of the idiomatic expressions, the sharp implications, add a touch of eager mischievousness. These are lasting virtues in any literature. Not all the poems of the *Flower of Lovers* are, of course, so attractive. The songbook, as a whole, is" (Joan Fuster, p. 41).

## III *Theater*

The only *autos sacramentales* (Eucharistic plays) in Catalan literature are the two written by Timoneda and known in that language as *El castell d'Emaús* (The Castle [i.e., Village] of Emmaus) and *L'església militant* (The Church Militant).[4] Both were first published in the *Ternario sacramental* (Valencia: Joan Navarro, 1575), which Timoneda dedicated to Juan de Ribera, Archbishop of Valencia from 1568 to 1611. The two plays are written in *quintillas*, a five-line octosyllabic stanza having two consonantal rhymes.

The Emmaus play is in part based, as Timoneda points out, on the episode described in the Gospel of St. Luke, Ch. 24, verses 13–35, wherein the risen Christ, for some time unrecognized, took supper with two disciples. This theme was widely popular in literature and the plastic arts.[5]

The characters are Juan González, an old innkeeper; Marimendrales, his wife; Antón the fool, their son; Human Desire, a shepherd; and five pilgrims: Christ, Luke, Cleopas, Pleasure, and Contentment.

The play opens with a sort of detachable *paso* (imitating one of Rueda's according to Mérimée)[6] in which the irascible González orders about his wife and son. As Luke and Cleopas walk along sadly discussing the recent death of Christ, the latter comes up to them in the guise of a pilgrim. He consoles them with His words and they invite Him to join them in the "Castle" of Emmaus. González and Antón serve the pilgrims bread and fruit. Christ suddenly disappears, leaving Luke and Cleopas convinced that He was the Messiah. The two now engage two other pilgrims in conversation; they are Pleasure and Contentment, who explain the spiritual significance of bread in the Old and New Testaments. Human Desire arrives and asks questions of a doctrinal nature about the divine bread "which is on the altar." The questions are answered by Luke, Cleopas, Contentment, and Pleasure. The play ends with a Eucharistic song.

Linguistically, this play is actually bilingual, for the following use Castilian: González, his wife, his son, and Human Desire, while Valencian is used by Christ, Luke, Cleopas, Contentment, and Pleasure, i.e., all the *pilgrims*. The Valencian-speakers of the play are the "noble" figures, as Batllori correctly observes, [7] whereas the Castilian-speakers play inferior or comic roles, a circumstance that doubtless did not pass unnoticed by the Valencian audience.

Structurally the play comprises three parts: (1) the detachable comic *paso*, (2) the biblically inspired encounter of the two disciples with the initially unrecognized Christ, and (3) the didactic conversation in which the two disciples participate with the allegorical figures Pleasure, Contentment, and Human Desire. In the seventeenth century, these same ingredients (comedy, allegory, and religious instruction), in different and more subtle mixes, characterized the sacramental plays of Calderón, the greatest exponent of this genre.

Chronologically, the play may be at least as old as 1569, when it was performed before Juan de Ribera according to Timoneda's dedicatory Epistle (but see below on the veracity of this statement).

Unlike the Emmaus play, *L'església militant* (The Church Militant) is written entirely in Valencian. If it was indeed performed before Juan de Ribera in 1569, as the dedicatory Epistle states, Timoneda must have retouched it—not unusual for him—since there are several references in this version to events that occurred after that date. For example, one of the characters is Pope Gregory XIII, who was not crowned pope until 1572. There is also an allusion to the Massacre of St. Bartholomew's Day, which took place in August, 1572. In any case, it is precisely the historical background of this play that gives it an added dimension of interest: a characteristic that would also mark this genre during the period of its greatest triumph in the seventeenth century.

The cast is made up of the following shepherds: Christ, Pope Gregory, King Philip, Opinion, St. Augustine, and St. Thomas, as well as the shepherdesses Church and Liberty.

The play opens with a speech by Church, the Spouse of Christ, lamenting her losses in England, France, and Germany, and praising the devotion of Spain in general and of Valencia in particular.

Christ appears and asks Church who is annoying her. She replies, "those treacherous Lutherans." Christ points out that she has powerful defenders: (Pope) Gregory XIII, Philip (II of Spain), and John (of Austria). He then leaves. The shepherds Gregory and Philip enter to console her for the loss of her sheep. Liberty and Opinion enter expressing their heretical ideas. Philip wishes to kill them but Church tries in vain to convert them. Philip hurls himself at Opinion. Augustine and Thomas enter and by their arguments convince Opinion and Liberty that they should obey Church. Opinion then inquires about the nature of the Eucharist whose feast is being celebrated on this day. Thomas and Augustine answer Opinion's questions and the play ends with a song of praise to the Church. *L'església militant* stands out among Timoneda's numerous surviving religious and secular works as the one that best reveals his awareness of a problem which greatly concerned his nation in the sixteenth century: the rise of Protestantism.

CHAPTER 9

# *Summation*

IF one quality characterizes Timoneda's oeuvre more than any other, it is diversity, both of genre and of theme. The Valencian belongs to the history of fiction and nonfiction, to literature and folklore, to Castilian as well as Catalan belles-lettres. His writings include the three major genres: prose fiction, poetry, and theater. In the first category he published *cuentos* (short stories), anecdotes, facetiae, and even a Milesian or Byzantine novelette (*patraña* XI). His poetry encompasses the lyrical, the narrative, the courtly, and the popular or traditional type, and such metrical forms as the ballad and the sonnet as well as *canciones, villancicos, motes, lamentaciones, chistes, endechas, enfados, adivinanzas,* etc. For the theater he produced realistic *entremeses,* allegorical *autos sacramentales,* and *comedias* involving fantasy, comedy, and tragedy. In addition, his theatrical compositions include several subgenres such as the detachable *paso,* the prologue, the Christmas and the Marian *auto,* and an allegorical colloquy.

Thematically, the same diversity obtains. Though the dominant themes are love, history, and religion, innumerable variations appear and many reappear. Among the recurrent themes are: the false accusation of sexual misconduct, look-alikes, Hero and Leander, Diego Moreno, *la morena,* and *la bella malmaridada.* Other subjects include the Cid, the Last Gothic King Roderick, Christ's Nativity and Crucifixion, color symbolism, Eucharistic allegory, and the infinite shades of lovers' emotions.

Timoneda's oeuvre embraces other aspects that are of interest to the investigator of proverbs, humor, Italian influence, onomastic devices, and the use of such printing formats as the *cancionero* (songbook), *romancero* (ballad collection), and the *pliego suelto* (chapbook).

The influence of individual works and genres has been noted at appropriate points throughout this book. Here I would like to quote Professor Avalle-Arce's elegantly stated appraisal of the overall significance of Timoneda's prose fiction and theater:

> The total work of Timoneda confronts us with a curious case: if we eliminate it, Spanish literature loses almost nothing from the viewpoint of esthetic achievement, but at the same time the conception of a good portion of later anecdotal-narrative and dramatic works would be difficult to explain. In other words, Timoneda is a great literary middleman. Both in his editions of the works of others and in his original books (if the term is valid when applied to this author), his work consists in gathering already elaborated artistic material and giving it the greatest possible diffusion thanks to his double activity as adaptor and bookseller. In this sense not the least of his merits is his treatment of folk literature. Timoneda collects popular themes, and polishes them a little, giving them a semi-artistic form, half-wrought but sufficient to confer on them a new rank that permits them to circulate in the world of letters, ready to be used to greater advantage" (pp. 16–17).[1]

It is in Timoneda's poetry—whether his own or rescued by him from oblivion—that the reader will find the "esthetic achievement" that Avalle-Arce misses in the Valencian's prose fiction and theater. There is hardly an anthology of Spanish Golden Age poetry that does not include some of Timoneda's lyrics, especially those of the traditional type. And this was true even before the recent attribution of the *Flor de enamorados* (Flower of Lovers) to the Valencian poet. For example, the anthology of Dámaso Alonso and J. M. Blecua contains nine of Timoneda's poems, all of which, they say, "seem to be [his] personal creations."[2] Two of their selections are deservedly among the most frequently anthologized of his lyrics: one is "Veo las ovejas," a shepherdess' love lament from the *Sarao de amor* (fol. 10v), which appears in Alin, Lapesa, Moreno Báez, E. A. Peers, and Sainz de Robles;[3] the other, also from the *Sarao de amor* (fol. 46v), is "Soy garridica," on the *bella malmaridada* theme, which is found in Alin (refrain only), Cohen (in Spanish and English),[4] Sainz de Robles, and Terry.[5]

Another delightful pastoral lyric with a long history as an anthologized poem is "¿Por qué olvidas el rebaño?" After its appearance in the *Enredo de amor* and a *pliego suelto*, it has merited inclusion in the following collections: *Flor de romances y glosas*

(1578), Böhl de Faber (1821–1825),[6] John Bowring (English translation based on preceding text),[7] Longfellow (the Bowring translation),[8] and Cejador.[9]

I imagine that some readers will share Allison Peers' opinion that precedes his two selections from Timoneda's poetry: "Neither in the majority of these [comedies and farces] nor in his anecdotal tales would one suspect him of being a poet and such graceful lyrics as those printed below come as a welcome surprise."[10]

Among all the reprints of his works and the copious scattered material related to him, whether laudatory or chary of praise, nothing, I suspect, would have pleased the Valencian bookseller more than two publishing events of recent occurrence. The first is the inclusion of an English translation of his *patraña* IV in the November, 1957, issue of the magazine *Playboy*. The translation by J. A. Gato was reprinted in a pocket book entitled *Playboy's Ribald Classics* (Chicago: Playboy Press, 1966). The other event is the appearance of his name on a series of narrative works (Colección Juan Timoneda [de narraciones españolas]) published by Papeles de Son Armadans of Madrid and Palma de Mallorca.

# *Notes and References*

## *Chapter One*

1. A commendable general history of this period is John Lynch's *Spain under the Habsburgs*, Vol. I: *Empire and Absolutism 1516–1598* (New York: Oxford University Press, 1964). Manuel Fernández Alvarez offers a sociological perspective in *La sociedad española del Renacimiento* (Salamanca: Anaya, 1970).

2. For all matters related to Valencia, see Francisco Almela y Vives, *Valencia y su reino* (Valencia: Ediciones Mariola, 1965).

3. In addition, there is a reference to the mineral wealth of Peru in *La oveja perdida* (ed. E. González Pedroso, *Biblioteca de autores españoles,* Vol. 58), p. 81a.

4. I. A. Leonard, *Books of the Brave* (reprint, New York: Gordian Press, 1964), p. 122.

5. Othón Arróniz, *La influencia italiana en el nacimiento de la comedia española* (Madrid: Gredos, 1969), p. 9.

6. Concerning censorship in Spain, see G. H. Putnam, *The Censorship of the Church of Rome,* 2 vols. (New York: B. Blom, 1967 [reprint of 1906 ed.]), II, 313–28; and, for a more balanced view, O. H. Green, *Spain and the Western Tradition,* 4 vols. (Madison and Milwaukee: University of Wisconsin Press, 1963–66), III, 457–66, and IV, Chapter V, esp. pp. 178–82. Putnam (I, 162) points out that the famous Index of Valdés of 1559 "is the first Spanish publication in which the lists represent original work on the part of the Spanish editors in the selection of literature to be condemned."

7. The Valencian dialect of the Catalan language is referred to as "Valencian" by some and as "Catalan" by others; I use "Catalan-Valencian" as a compromise between the two designations.

8. See Manuel Carboneres, *Picaronas y alcahuetes o la mancebía de Valencia* (Valencia: El Mercantil, 1876).

9. On the controversial history of printing in fifteenth-century Spain, see A. Millares Carlo, *Introducción a la historia del libro y de las bibliotecas* (México: Fondo de Cultura Económica, 1971), pp. 101–12.

10. See N. D. Shergold, *A History of the Spanish Stage* (Oxford: Clarendon Press, 1967), pp. 194–95.

*Chapter Two*

1. The documents related to Timoneda's life are printed in J. E. Serrano y Morales, *Reseña histórica en forma de diccionario de las imprentas que han existido en Valencia* (Valencia: Imprenta de F. Domenech, 1898–99) and in F. Martí Grajales, *Ensayo de un diccionario biográfico y bibliográfico de los poetas que florecieron en el reino de Valencia hasta el año 1700* (Madrid: Tip. de la "Revista de Archivos, Bibliotecas y Museos," 1927). More recently, they have been reprinted in *Obras de Juan de Timoneda,* [ed. Eduardo Juliá Martínez], Sociedad de Bibliófilos Españoles, Segunda Época, Tomos 19, 21, 22 (3 vols., Madrid: Aldus, 1947–48), I, xxix–li.

2. The famous seventeenth-century bibliographer Nicolás Antonio listed among Timoneda's publications a *Silva de varias canciones* (Seville: Alfonso [Alonso] de la Barrera, 1511). On the basis of this 1511 date some investigators assume that the Valencian author must have been born around 1490 or before. Such an early date would make understandable Cervantes' comment in 1582 (?) about Timoneda who "in age conquers Time" (*Los baños de Argel,* Act III). However, most bibliographers now believe that the date 1511 is a misprint for 1571 (or 1581 or 1591), in view of the fact that a printer named Alonso de la Barrera is known to have been working in Seville between 1569 and 1599 (Francisco Escudero y Perosso, *Tipografía hispalense* [Madrid: "Sucesores de Rivadeneyra," 1894], p. 29 and no. 858) whereas the existence of a Sevillan printer of that name cannot be documented in 1511. No copy of the book in question exists today. The more widely accepted date of birth, 1518–1520, leaves unexplained Cervantes' aforementioned comment.

3. See Vicente Castañeda, *Antecedentes y notas sobre la encuadernación valenciana en los siglos XVI y XVII* (Madrid: Imprenta y Editorial Maestre, 1949), p. 15.

4. On Rueda's visit to Valencia in 1560 and the possibility that he was there on other occasions, see Paul Russell-Gebbett, "Valencian in the Sixth *Paso* of Lope de Rueda's *Deleitoso,*" *Hispanic Review,* 21 (1953), 216–17.

5. Such is the assumption, for example, of E. Juliá Martínez in his edition of Timoneda's works cited in note 1; see III, Observaciones preliminares, xvi.

6. Federico Ruiz Morcuende, ed.: Timoneda, *El patrañuelo,* 4th ed., (Madrid: Espasa-Calpe, 1973; Clásicos Castellanos #101; [1st ed., 1930]), p. xiii. Hereafter the name Ruiz Morcuende and a page reference in the text will be used to refer to this 1973 edition.

7. Rinaldo Froldi, *Lope de Vega y la formación de la comedia. En torno a la tradición dramática valenciana y al primer teatro de Lope* (Salamanca: Anaya, 1968), p. 90.

8. The Inventory was printed by J. E. Serrano y Morales, *Reseña histórica,* pp. 548–55, and reprinted by E. Juliá Martínez, *Obras de Juan de Timoneda,* I, xl–li. Inadvertently omitted from the latter reprinting are the

following two entries: "Item hun llibre padilla dels de seuilla en nou sous" (Serrano y Morales, p. 550) and "Item Trenta doctrines a tres plechs tenen tres mans y quinze fulls" (Serrano y Morales, p. 554). The Inventory includes works by such celebrated authors as Alonso de Ercilla, Gaspar Gil Polo, Luis de Granada, Antonio de Guevara, Ausias March, Pedro Mexía (Mejía), Juan de Mena, Alonso de Orozco, Lope de Rueda, Timoneda himself, Antonio de Torquemada, Bartolomé de Torres Naharro, and Juan Luis Vives. Among the most represented genres in the list are histories, novels of chivalry, and pious works, including a copy of the *Doctrina cristiana* (1st ed., 1548) by the controversial Doctor Constantino Ponce de la Fuente.

9. Pedro Salvá y Mallén, *Catálogo de la biblioteca de Salvá*, 2 vols. (Valencia: Imprenta de Ferrer de Orga, 1872 [reprint, Barcelona: Porter-Libros, 1963]).

10. Bartolomé José Gallardo, *Ensayo de una biblioteca española de libros raros y curiosos*, 4 vols. (Madrid: Rivadeneyra, 1863–89 [reprint, Madrid: Gredos, 1968]).

11. See J. E. Serrano y Morales, *Reseña histórica*, p. 541.

12. For the passage in question, see the edition of José Rojas Garcidueñas (México: El Colegio de México, 1950), p. 49 (fol. 30 recto).

## *Chapter Three*

1. *Sobremesa* will be used as an abbreviation of *El sobremesa y alivio de caminantes* (Valencia: Joan Navarro, 1569; facsimile ed., Madrid, 1917), the most complete version of the collection of anecdotes that first began to appear in 1563.

2. Walter Pabst, *La novela corta en la teoría y en la creación literaria* (Madrid: Gredos, 1972), p. 55.

3. See Gracián Dantisco's *Galateo español*, ed. M. Morreale (Madrid: Consejo Superior de Investigaciones Científicas, 1968), pp. 153–54.

4. William Nelson, *Fact or Fiction: The Dilemma of the Renaissance Storyteller* (Cambridge, Mass.: Harvard University Press, 1973), esp. Chapter 3.

5. Sherman H. Eoff, "The *Patrañuelo* of Juan de Timoneda. An Edition with Introduction and Notes," dissertation, University of Chicago, 1929, p. 17. Hereafter the name Eoff and a page reference in the text will be used to refer to this dissertation.

6. Marcelino Menéndez y Pelayo, *Orígenes de la novela*, ed. E. Sánchez Reyes, 4 vols. (Madrid-Santander: Consejo Superior de Investigaciones Científicas, 2nd ed., 1962), III, 67. Hereafter the name Menéndez y Pelayo plus a page reference in the text will be used to refer to this frequently cited work. Any other reference to Menéndez y Pelayo will be appropriately footnoted.

7. Rudolph Schevill, ed., "*El buen aviso y portacuentos* by Juan Timoneda," *Revue Hispanique*, 24 (1911), 175.

8. Mariano Baquero Goyanes, ed.: Juan Timoneda, *El patrañuelo* (Madrid: E.M.E.S.A., 1968), p. 23. Hereafter the name Baquero Goyanes and a page reference in the text will be used to refer to this edition.

9. P. N. Dunn, *Castillo Solórzano and the Decline of the Spanish Novel* (Oxford: Basil Blackwell, 1952), p. 3.

10. Quoted in Edward Storer, trans., *The Facetiae of Poggio and Other Medieval Story-Tellers* (New York: E. P. Dutton, [1928]), p. 31.

11. Charles Speroni, *Wit and Wisdom of the Italian Renaissance* (Berkeley and Los Angeles: University of California Press, 1964), pp. 8–9. Hereafter the name Speroni and a page reference in the text will be used to refer to this work.

12. *Playboy*, Vol. 21, No. 8 (August, 1974), 131.

13. *La Estafeta Literaria*, Núm. 540 (May 15, 1974), 46.

14. Quoted in F. Rodríguez Marín, ed.: Cervantes, *Rinconete y Cortadillo*, 2nd ed. (Madrid: Tipografía de la "Rev. de Archivos, Bibliotecas y Museos," 1920), p. 153, n. 1.

15. See the "Prólogo Sumario de ambos los tomos" of *La pícara Justina* (Medina del Campo, 1605).

16. See his *Corte na aldea e noites de inverno* (Lisboa: Pedro Crasbeeck, 1619), folio 110 verso.

17. See José M. Bella, ed.: Mira de Amescua, *La mesonera del cielo* (Madrid: Espasa-Calpe, 1972), p. 7 and n. to v. 99.

18. Quoted in Othón Arróniz, *La influencia italiana*, p. 72.

19. D. P. Rotunda, *Motif-Index of the Italian Novella in Prose* (Bloomington: Indiana University, 1942), p. 109 (K1514.4.1). Subsequent references to Rotunda are to be understood as references to this *Motif-Index*. For a "psychological" interpretation of this famous tale, see G. Legman, *Rationale of the Dirty Joke: An Analysis of Sexual Humor* (New York: Evergreen Black Cat Edition, 1971), pp. 18–19 and 736.

20. Apparently this symbolism is still understood in the United States; see p. 107 of the issue of *Playboy* cited in note 12.

21. Henri Recoules, "Cervantes y Timoneda y los entremeses del siglo XVII," *Boletín de la Biblioteca de Menéndez Pelayo*, 48 (1972), 246–47.

22. Juan B. Rael, *Cuentos Españoles de Colorado y Nuevo Méjico*, 2 vols. (Stanford, Calif.: Stanford University Press, [1957?]), p. 8.

23. James Geddes, Jr., ed.: Calderón, *El alcalde de Zalamea* (Boston: D. C. Heath, 1918), p. 143, n. to vv. 926–28.

24. On the literary manifestations of this custom, see María Rosa Lida de Malkiel, *La originalidad artística de "La Celestina"* (Buenos Aires: EUDEBA, 1962), p. 694, note.

25. José María Iribarren, for example, seems to take Timoneda's words

literally; see *El porqué de los dichos*, 3rd ed. (Madrid: Aguilar, 1962), pp. 125, 546.

26. Headings of this type do not appear in the edition of Valencia, 1569; they are used, however, in the edition of Alcalá, 1576.

27. A. González Palencia, "Con la ilusión basta" in the author's *Historias y leyendas: Estudios literarios* (Madrid: Consejo Superior de Investigaciones Científicas, 1942), pp. 145–60. Cf. Fernando de la Granja, "Cuentos árabes en 'El sobremesa' de Timoneda," *Al-Andalus*, 34 (1969), esp. pp. 384–88.

28. See Eric Partridge, *Shakespeare's Bawdy*, rev. ed. (New York: E. P. Dutton, 1969), s.v. *cuckold* and *cuckoo*.

29. See Bernardino Daza Pinciano, trans., *Los emblemas de Alciato* (Lyon: Mathia Bonhome, 1549), p. 173.

30. Rodrigo Caro, *Días geniales o lúdicros* (Sevilla: Impr. de El Mercantil Sevillano, 1884; Sociedad de Bibliófilos Andaluces, 1a Ser., XV), pp. 217–23.

31. For a less subtle Arabic variant of this anecdote, see Tomás García Figueras, ed., *Cuentos de Yehá* (Jerez de la Frontera: "Nueva Litografía Jerezana," 1934), p. 189, no. 333.

32. Theodor Rosebury, *Life on Man* (New York: Viking, 1969), Ch. 12. Mention should be made also of the important study on literary scatology by Jae Num Lee, *Swift and Scatological Satire* (Albuquerque: University of New Mexico Press, 1971); see esp. Ch. 1 entitled "Scatology in Continental Satirical Writings from Aristophanes to Rabelais."

33. G. Legman, "On Sexual Speech and Slang," in *Dictionary of Slang and Its Analogues Past and Present*, compiled and edited by J. S. Farmer and W. E. Henley, rev. ed. (New Hyde Park, N.Y.: University Books, 1966), I, lxiv.

34. Paul D. Zimmerman in *Newsweek*, October 8, 1973, p. 100.

35. Rudolph Schevill, "*El buen aviso*," p. 172, doubts the existence of the editions of 1569 and 1570.

36. *Ibid.*, p. 174.

37. Anselmo de Legarda, *Lo vizcaíno en la literatura castellana* (San Sebastián: Biblioteca Vascongada de los Amigos del País, 1953), p. 286.

38. William S. Hendrix, *Some Native Comic Types in the Early Spanish Drama* (Columbus, Ohio: Ohio State University, Contributions in Languages and Literatures, No. 1, 1925), p. 26.

39. Concerning the two anecdotes in the *Sobremesa*, see Albert Mas, *Les Turcs dans la littérature espagnole du Siècle d'Or*, 2 vols. (Paris: Centre de Recherches Hispaniques, Institut d'Études Hispaniques, 1967), I, 164.

40. Cf. Hendrix, *Some Native Comic Types*, pp. 20–22.

41. See Rotunda, p. 57 (J1367) and p. 134 (K2052.4.2.).

42. Schevill, "*El buen aviso*," p. 177.

43. In his edition of the *Poema de mio Cid,* 6th ed. corr. (Madrid: Espasa-Calpe, 1951; Clásicos Castellanos #24), pp. 28–30.

44. See Xavier A. Fernández's edition of *Tan largo me lo fiáis* (Madrid: Revista "Estudios", 1967) and Professor Wade's review-article on this work, in *Bulletin of the Comediantes,* 20 (1968), No. 2, 31–42.

45. "Una anécdota folklórica del *tan largo me lo fiáis* no notada hasta la fecha," *Revista de Filología Hispánica,* 4 (1942), 70–72.

46. "More on Timoneda's *Tan Largo Me Lo Fiáis* Story and *El Burlador de Sevilla,*" *Revista de Estudios Hispánicos,* 4 (1970), 107–12.

47. Schevill, "*El buen aviso,*" p. 179.

48. Homero Serís, *Guía de nuevos temas de literatura española,* ed. D. W. McPheeters (New York: Hispanic Society of America, 1973), p. 192.

49. Giorgio Valli, "Las fuentes italianas de la Patraña IX de Timoneda," *Revista de Filología Española,* 30 (1946), 369–81.

50. Concerning this "peculiar technique of deriving the title [of a play] directly as an adjective from the chief character," see J. E. Gillet, ed., *Propalladia and Other Works of Bartolomé de Torres Naharro,* 4 vols. (Bryn Mawr and Philadelphia: University of Pennsylvania Press, 1943–61), IV, 234.

51. See "Tres comedias de Alonso de la Vega" in his *Estudios y discursos de crítica histórica y literaria,* ed. E. Sánchez Reyes, 7 vols. (Madrid and Santander: Consejo Superior de Investigaciones Científicas, 1942), II, 389–96.

52. Menéndez y Pelayo, "Tres comedias," p. 394.

53. *Ibid.,* p. 389.

54. C. B. Bourland, "Boccaccio and the Decameron in Castilian and Catalan Literature," *Revue Hispanique,* 12 (1905), 163–88.

55. "New Light on the Origin of the Griselda Story," *Texas Studies in Literature and Language,* 13 (1971), 153–208.

56. In his edition of the *Patrañuelo* (Madrid: Castilla, 1948), p. 216, n. 20.

57. Rafael Ferreres, ed.: Timoneda, *El patrañuelo,* (Madrid: Castalia, 1971), p. 65. Subsequent references to Professor Ferreres are to be understood as references to this edition.

58. The best edition is that of Hermann Oesterley (Hildesheim: Georg Olm, 1963 [reprint of ed. Berlin, 1872]). The *Gesta Romanorum* is also available in an English version with numeration somewhat different from Oesterley's: translated by Charles Swan, revised and corrected by Wynnard Hooper (New York: AMS Press, 1970 [reprint of ed. London, 1894]). Where they are different, both the Oesterley and Swan-Hooper chapter numbers will be given.

59. Felix Liebrecht, *John Dunlop's Geschichte der Prosadichtungen* (Berlin: G.W.F. Müller, 1851), p. 500.

60. Pedro Salvá y Mallén, *Catálogo de la biblioteca de Salvá,* 2 vols. (Valencia: Imprenta de Ferrer de Orga, 1872 [reprint, Barcelona: Porter-Libros, 1963]), II, 186a.

61. Valli, "Las fuentes italianas," p. 372, footnote.

62. Antonio Gasparetti, "Sulla fonte italiana della Patraña VI di Juan de Timoneda," *Letterature Moderne,* 2 (1951), 79–80.

63. Enrico Cerulli, *Il "Patrañuelo" di Juan Timoneda e l'elemento arabo nella novella italiana e spagnola del Rinascimento* (Roma, 1955; in Atti dell' Accademia Nazionale dei Lincei. Memorie. Classe di scienze morali, storiche e filologiche. Ser. 8. Vol. 7. Fasc. 3).

64. *Ibid.*, p. 180, n. 2.

65. Bartolomé José Gallardo, *Ensayo de una biblioteca española de libros raros y curiosos,* 4 vols. (Madrid: Rivadeneyra, 1863–89 [reprint, Madrid: Gredos, 1968]), III, 738. But this view is open to serious question; see F. Márquez Villanueva, *Fuentes literarias cervantinas* (Madrid: Gredos, 1973), p. 165, n. 68.

66. F. Rodríguez Marín, ed.: Cervantes, *Don Quijote,* 10 vols. (Madrid: Atlas, 1947–49), VII, 26.

67. Menéndez y Pelayo, in his 1905 essay on Alonso de la Vega reprinted as indicated in note 51; Menéndez Pidal, cited in Menéndez y Pelayo, *Orígenes,* III, 85; Valli, "Las fuentes italianas"; Arróniz, *La influencia italiana.*

68. Valli, "Las fuentes italianas," p. 374.

69. F. J. Wolf and C. Hofmann, eds., *Primavera y flor de romances,* 2 vols. (Berlin: Asher, 1856).

70. See Eoff, pp. 87–89.

71. Eugenio Asensio, *Itinerario del entremés* (Madrid: Gredos, 2nd ed. rev., 1971), pp. 28–29.

72. Recoules, "Cervantes y Timoneda," pp. 247–250.

73. Serís, *Nuevo ensayo de una biblioteca española de libros raros y curiosos* (New York: Hispanic Society of America, 1964), I, 80–115.

74. Albert H. Smyth, *Shakespeare's Pericles and Apollonius of Tyre: A Study in Comparative Literature* (Philadelphia: MacCalla, 1898 [reprint, New York: AMS Press, 1972]), p. 5.

75. Recoules, "Cervantes y Timoneda," pp. 238–43. It is interesting to note that this *patraña* XII as well as numbers X and VI are cited as examples of the facetia in the doctoral dissertation of Clifford Alan Soons, "The Traditions of the Facetia and the Jest-book in the Spanish Peninsula, from the Introduction of Printing to about 1750" (Harvard University, 1971). For Dr. Soons, "The essence of the facetia is best observed in the variety of its cases, which fall into two principal categories: the triumph of a trickster over his dupe, and the equalizing of the fortunes of both trickster and his dupe" (p. 2). Accordingly, Soons does not deal with Timoneda's *Sobremesa* and

*Buen aviso.* On the other hand, as will be recalled, in the present work the term facetia is used in conformity with Charles Speroni's description of the genre; see p. 23.

76. See Eoff, pp. 123–25.

77. Aurelio M. Espinosa, *Cuentos populares españoles*, 3 vols. (Madrid: Consejo Superior de Investigaciones Científicas, 1946–47), II, 101–11.

78. In his study entitled *Some Forms of the Riddle Question and the Exercise of the Wits in Popular Fiction and Formal Literature* (University of California Publications in Modern Philology, Vol. 2, No. 3, pp. 183–237, November 2, 1911).

79. Dan Ben-Amos, "The Americanization of 'The King and the Abbot,'" *Indiana Folklore*, 2 (1969), 115–23.

80. In the collection described above in note 22.

81. See Eoff, pp. 131–35.

82. Elise Richter, "Juan Timoneda und das Imogen-Portia-Motiv," *Shakespeare-Jahrbuch*, 64 (1928), 141–58.

83. E. B. Place, *María de Zayas, an Outstanding Woman Short-story Writer of Seventeenth-Century Spain* (The University of Colorado Studies, Vol. XIII, No. 1, 1923, pp. 1–56), pp. 30–32.

84. M. F. Galiano, "Sobre la evolución de la leyenda de Ciro en nuestros siglos XVI y XVII," *Estudios Clásicos*, 6 (1961), 93–98.

85. *Gesta Romanorum:* Ch. 283 in ed. H. Oesterley; no. 98 on pp. l–liii of Introduction in ed. Swan-Hooper.

86. Cerulli, *Il "Patrañuelo,"* pp. 99–169.

87. For a very similar Arabic folktale, see the collection cited in note 31, pp. 73–76, no. 121.

88. This is no. 101 on pp. liii–lx of Introduction in ed. Swan-Hooper.

89. In the work cited in note 83, pp. 48–52.

90. J. B. Avalle-Arce, "Una tradición literaria: el cuento de los dos amigos," *Nueva Revista de Filología Hispánica*, 11 (1957), 1–35.

91. *Ibid.*, p. 34.

92. E. Mérimée and S. G. Morley, *A History of Spanish Literature* (New York: Holt, 1930), p. 328.

93. F. De Haan, "Barlaam and Joasaph in Spain," *Modern Language Notes*, 10 (1895), cols. 138–39.

94. Asensio, *Itinerario del entremés*, pp. 26–29.

95. Buchanan, "Short Stories and Anecdotes in Spanish Plays," *Modern Language Review*, 4 (1908–09), 178–84; 5 (1910), 78–89. The quotation is from vol. 4, p. 179.

96. Edmond Cros, *Contribution à l'étude des sources de Guzmán de Alfarache* [Montpellier, 1967], p. 107; Donald McGrady, *Mateo Alemán* (New York: Twayne, 1968), p. 138.

97. J. W. Childers, *A Study of Sources and Analogues of the "Cuentos"*

*in Alcalá Yáñez' "Alonso, mozo de muchos amos"* (Chicago: Private Edition, 1941), p. 3, no. 29.

98. Mérimée and Morley, *Spanish Literature,* p. 328.

*Chapter Four*

1. Erik v. Kraemer, *Le type du faux mendiant dans les littératures romanes depuis le moyen âge jusqu'au XVII^e siècle* (Helsingfors: Societas Scientiarum Fennica, 1944), pp. 307–11.
2. Leandro Fernández de Moratín, *Orígenes del teatro español,* ed. B. C. Aribau *(Biblioteca de autores españoles,* Vol. 2), p. 204a.
3. *Ibid.*
4. J. P. Wickersham Crawford, *Spanish Drama before Lope de Vega,* rev. ed. (Philadelphia: University of Pennsylvania Press, 1967), p. 129. Hereafter the name Crawford and a page reference in the text will be used to refer to this work.
5. Emilio Cotarelo y Mori, ed., *Colección de entremeses, loas, bailes, jácaras y mojigangas . . . (Nueva biblioteca de autores españoles,* Vols. 17, 18; Madrid: Bailly-Bailliére, 1911), Tomo I, Vol. 1, p. lxii.
6. In *La Comédie espagnole de Lope de Rueda,* trad. de A. Germond de Lavigne (Paris: L. Michaud, 1883), pp. 193–207.
7. Cotarelo, *Colección de entremeses,* p. lxii.
8. Eugenio Asensio, *Itinerario del entremés* (Madrid: Gredos, 2nd rev. ed., 1971), pp. 41–42.
9. E. Juliá Martínez, "Originalidad de Timoneda," *Revista Valenciana de Filología,* 5 (1955–1958), 91–151.
10. E. González Pedroso, ed., *Autos sacramentales desde su origen hasta fines del siglo XVII (Biblioteca de autores españoles,* Vol. 58), p. 77.
11. Bruce W. Wardropper, *Introducción al teatro religioso del Siglo de Oro: Evolución del auto sacramental antes de Calderón* (Salamanca: Anaya, 1967), p. 272.
12. Juliá Martínez, "Originalidad," p. 97.
13. Concerning this conventional pastoral speech, see John Lihani, *El lenguaje de Lucas Fernández; Estudio del dialecto sayagués* (Bogotá: Instituto Caro y Cuervo, 1973).
14. In the edition by E. Juliá Martínez cited in note 1 to Chapter 2.
15. Jean-Louis Flecniakoska, *La formation de l'auto religieux en Espagne avant Calderón (1550–1635)* ([Montpellier: Imprimerie Paul Dehan], 1961), p. 35.
16. E. González Pedroso, ed., *Autos sacramentales,* p. 97a.
17. *Ibid.*, p. 99a.
18. Léo Rouanet, ed., *Colección de autos, farsas y coloquios del siglo XVI,* 4 vols. (Barcelona: "L'Avenç," 1901).
19. Wardropper, *Introducción al teatro religioso,* p. 246.
20. Holland Peterson, "*Amphitrión* and *Los Menemnos:* An Edition of

the First Two Plays of Juan Timoneda's *Las tres comedias,* with an Introduction on Plautine Influence," dissertation, University of Toronto, 1961. I quote from the abstract, which I have on microfilm along with the dissertation.

21. Peterson, "*Amphitrión* and *Los Menemnos.*" Again I quote from the abstract on microfilm.

22. Sue-Lin Chow, "Another Source for Timoneda's *Menemnos,*" *Bulletin of the Comediantes,* 21 (1969), 52–56.

23. The correct name "Carmelia" appears in all but three places (including the title page), where "Cornelia" is used.

24. Othón Arróniz, *La influencia italiana,* p. 142.

25. In the edition of E. Juliá Martínez, Vol. III.

26. See Serrano y Morales, *Reseña histórica,* p. 550.

27. In the edition of E. Juliá Martínez, Vol. III.

28. Joseph E. Gillet, "Torres Naharro and the Spanish Drama of the Sixteenth Century," in *Estudios eruditos in memoriam de Adolfo Bonilla y San Martín* (Madrid, 1930), II, 437–68.

29. Giuseppina Ledda, "Sulla *Turiana* di Juan de Timoneda," *Miscellanea di studi ispanici,* No. 14 (1966–67), 150–169.

30. Rinaldo Froldi, *Lope de Vega,* p. 91.

31. J. M. Regueiro, "Juan Timoneda y la tradición dramática española," *Dissertation Abstracts International-Humanities,* Vol. 33A, Nos. 10–12 (1973), p. 6882A.

## *Chapter Five*

1. A. Rodríguez-Moñino, *Las series valencianas del romancero nuevo y los cancionerillos de Munich (1589–1602)* (Valencia: Diputación Provincial, 1963), p. 31.

2. Rodríguez-Moñino, *Poesía y cancioneros (siglo XVI)* (Madrid: Real Academia Española, 1968), p. 85. In my analysis of the *Sarao de amor* I shall follow Rodríguez-Moñino's proposal (p. 84) as to the makeup of the book's two *partes.*

3. *Ibid.*

4. M. Frenk Alatorre, *Entre folklore y literatura (Lírica hispánica antigua)* (México: El Colegio de México, 1971), p. 19.

5. Otis H. Green, *Spain and the Western Tradition,* I, 95–96.

6. *Sarao de amor,* fol. 47r.

7. *Ibid.,* fol. 48r–v.

8. Arthur Terry, ed., *An Anthology of Spanish Poetry 1500–1700,* 2 vols. (Oxford: Pergamon, 1965–68), I, 75.

9. Rodríguez-Moñino, *Manual bibliográfico de cancioneros y romanceros (siglo XVI),* 2 vols. (Madrid: Castalia, 1973).

10. There is a modern reprint of this edition with an *Estudio preliminar* by A. Rodríguez-Moñino and D. Devoto (Valencia; Castalia, 1954).

11. Josep Romeu i Figueras, *Joan Timoneda i la "Flor de enamorados," cançoner bilingüe. Un estudi i una aportació bibliogràfica* (Barcelona: Reial Acadèmia de Bones Lletres, 1972). His analysis of the *Flor's partes* and sections will be followed in my discussion. Hereafter the name Romeu and a page reference in the text will be used to refer to this work.

12. Joan Fuster, ed.: Timoneda, *Flor d'enamorats* (Valencia: Albatros, 1973).

13. The myth also inspired a movie entitled *Pope Joan* starring Liv Ullmann in the title role and Trevor Howard as Pope Leo IV; for details, see the review in *Time,* September 11, 1972, pp. 78 and 80.

14. Pedro Salvá y Mallén, *Catálogo de la biblioteca de Salvá,* 2 vols. (Valencia: Imprenta de Ferrer de Orga, 1872 [reprint, Barcelona: Porter-Libros, 1963]), I, 171a.

15. Amelia Agostini de del Río, ed., *Flores del romancero* (Englewood Cliffs: Prentice-Hall, 1970), p. 1.

16. J. M. Gómez-Tabanera, ed., *El folklore español* (Madrid: Instituto Español de Antropología Aplicada, 1968), pp. 87–88.

17. C. C. Smith, in his review of Rodríguez-Moñino and Devoto's reprint of Timoneda's *Rosas de romances,* in *Bulletin of Hispanic Studies,* 41 (1964), 265.

18. Rodríguez-Moñino, *Diccionario bibliográfico de pliegos sueltos poéticos (siglo XVI)* (Madrid: Castalia, 1970), p. 11.

19. *Ibid.*

20. Bartolomé José Gallardo, *Ensayo de una biblioteca española de libros raros y curiosos,* 4 vols. (Madrid: Rivadeneyra, 1863–89 [reprint, Madrid: Gredos, 1968]), nos. 4035 and 4036.

21. The volumes and pages are: 3 (1916), 564–70; 5 (1918) 506–10; 7 (1920), 86–95.

*Chapter Six*

1. Emilio Cotarelo y Mori, *Lope de Rueda y el teatro español de su tiempo* (Madrid: Imprenta de "La Revista Española," 1901), p. 30, n. 3.

2. Juliá Martínez, ed.: Timoneda, *Obras,* I, xiii.

3. Serrano y Morales, *Reseña histórica,* p. 552.

4. Edmund de Chasca, *Lope de Rueda's Comedia de Los Engañados: An Edition* (Chicago: Private Edition, 1941), p. 156, n. 8.

5. Juliá Martínez, ed.: Timoneda, *Obras,* I, xii.

6. See his edition of Lope de Rueda's *Eufemia* and *Armelina* (Salamanca and Madrid: Anaya, 1967), pp. 22–23, 39, et passim, and his edition of Lope de Rueda's *Los engañados* and *Medora* (Madrid: Espasa-Calpe, 1973; Clásicos Castellanos, #181), pp. xi, lii, liv, et passim. Not yet available is his "Catalanismos e intervención de Timoneda en las comedias de Lope de Rueda," a paper read at the Cuarto Congreso Internacional de Hispanistas, Salamanca, 1971.

### *Chapter Seven*

1. Justo Pastor Fuster, *Biblioteca valenciana,* 2 vols. (Valencia: Imp. y libr. de J. Ximeno, 1827–30), I, 164b; Martí Grajales, *Ensayo de un diccionario,* p. 450; A. Palau y Dulcet, *Manual del librero hispano-americano,* 2nd ed. (Barcelona and Oxford, 1948), XXIII, 187b.
2. An especially interesting study of this theme is found in Maurice Vloberg, *L'Eucharistie dans l'art,* 2 vols. (Grenoble and Paris: B. Arthaud, 1946), II, 208–14.
3. Francisco Vindel, *Manual gráfico-descriptivo del bibliófilo hispano-americano (1475–1850),* 12 vols. (Madrid: Imprenta Góngora, 1930–34), IX, 267–68.
4. Fray Juan Ruiz de Larrinaga, "Curiosidad bibliográfica. Impresos en Vizcaya, Guipúzcoa y Alava hasta el año 1901," in *Homenaje a D. Julio de Urquijo e Ybarra* (San Sebastián, 1949), II, 49–110.
5. H. J. R. Murray, *A History of Board-Games Other Than Chess* (Oxford: Clarendon Press, 1952), p. 78.

### *Chapter Eight*

1. The *Biblioteca de autores españoles* reading has been emended to conform to the facsimile edition of the Valencia 1569 printing. In English translation the saying is: "Let each one weep for his trouble in his own crucible."
2. The anthology is cited in note 12 to Chapter 5; hereinafter referred to simply by the editor's name.
3. Romeu's study is cited in note 11 to Chapter 5.
4. See *The "Aucto del castillo de Emaus" and the "Aucto de la Iglesia" of Juan Timoneda,* edited with introduction, notes, and translation into English by Mildred E. Johnson (University of Iowa Studies, Spanish Language and Literature, No. 4, 1933).
5. *Ibid.*, pp. 10–11; Maurice Vloberg, *L'Eucharistie dans l'art,* 2 vols. (Grenoble and Paris: B. Arthaud, 1946), I, 125–33; and Manuel Trens, *La eucaristía en el arte español* (Barcelona: Aymá, 1952), pp. 102–06.
6. Henri Mérimée, *L'art dramatique à Valencia* (Toulouse: Édouard Privat, 1913), p. 198.
7. J. M. Batllori, ed.: Timoneda, *L'església militant, El castell d'Emaús* (Barcelona: Edicions 62, 1967), p. 7.

### *Chapter Nine*

1. The quotation is from his study cited in note 90 to Chapter 3.
2. Dámaso Alonso and José M. Blecua, eds., *Antología de la poesía española: Poesía de tipo tradicional* (Madrid: Gredos, 1956), pp. 168–72 and 237–38.

3. José María Alin, ed., *El cancionero español de tipo tradicional* (Madrid: Taurus, 1968); Rafael Lapesa, ed., *Poetas del siglo XVI: Período clásico (1525–1590)* (Barcelona: Rauter, 1947); Enrique Moreno Báez, ed., *Antología de la poesía lírica española* (Madrid: Revista de Occidente, 1952); E. A. Peers, ed., *A Critical Anthology of Spanish Verse* (reprint, New York: Greenwood, 1968); F. C. Sainz de Robles, ed., *Historia y antología de la poesía española*, 2 vols., 5th ed. (Madrid: Aguilar, 1967).

4. J. M. Cohen, ed., *The Penguin Book of Spanish Verse* (1956).

5. Arthur Terry, in the anthology cited in note 8 to Chapter 5.

6. Juan Nicolás Böhl de Faber, ed., *Floresta de rimas antiguas castellanas*, 3 vols. (Hamburg: Perthes y Besser, 1821–25).

7. John Bowring, ed., *Ancient Poetry and Romances of Spain* (London: Taylor and Hessey, 1824).

8. Henry W. Longfellow, ed., *The Poets and Poetry of Europe*, rev. and enl. ed. (Boston: Houghton, Mifflin, [1896]).

9. Julio Cejador y Frauca, ed., *La verdadera poesía castellana: Floresta de la antigua lírica popular*, 5 vols. (Madrid: Tip. de la "Rev. de Arch., Bibl. y Museos," 1921–24).

10. Peers, *A Critical Anthology*, p. 203.

# *Selected Bibliography*

## PRIMARY SOURCES

The extremely rare original editions are cited here only where no modern reprint exists.


ARIBAU, BUENAVENTURA C., ed. *Novelistas anteriores a Cervantes. Biblioteca de autores españoles.* Vol. 3. Includes *El patrañuelo, Doce cuentos de Juan Aragonés,* and *El sobremesa y alivio de caminantes* (Parts I and II).

FOULCHÉ-DELBOSC, R., ed. "Les *romancerillos* de la Bibliothèque Ambrosienne." *Revue Hispanique,* 45 (1919). Includes the title poem of the *Cancionero llamado Dechado de colores* on pages 601–05.

GONZÁLEZ PEDROSO, E., ed. *Autos sacramentales desde su origen hasta fines del siglo XVII. Biblioteca de autores españoles,* Vol. 58. Includes the *autos sacramentales* that comprise the *[Primer] ternario sacramental* and the *Segundo ternario sacramental* except the two in Catalan-Valencian.

[JULIÁ MARTÍNEZ, E.], ed. *Obras de Juan de Timoneda.* Sociedad de Bibliófilos Españoles, Segunda Época, Tomos 19, 21, 22. 3 vols. Madrid: Aldus, 1947–48. The contents of this limited edition are as follows: Vol. I: *El patrañuelo, El sobremesa y alivio de caminantes* (Parts I and II), *El buen aviso y portacuentos* (Parts I and II); Vol. II: *Ternario espiritual, [Primer] ternario sacramental, Segundo ternario sacramental, Tres comedias;* Vol. III: *Turiana.*

RODRÍGUEZ-MOÑINO, A., ed. Timoneda, *Cancioneros llamados Enredo de amor, Guisadillo de amor y El truhanesco.* Valencia: Castalia, 1951. Reprint of the texts of 1573, together with an important bibliography of Timoneda's poetic production.

RODRÍGUEZ-MOÑINO, A., and D. Devoto, eds. *Cancionero llamado Flor de enamorados (Barcelona 1562).* Valencia: Castalia, 1954. Reprint of the 1562 edition, with an Introduction.

———. *Rosas de romances por Juan Timoneda (Valencia, 1573).* Valencia: Castalia, 1963. Reprint of the 1573 texts of *Rosa de amores, Rosa española, Rosa gentil,* and *Rosa real.*

SCHEVILL, RUDOLPH, ed. "*El buen aviso y portacuentos* by Juan Timoneda." *Revue Hispanique*, 24 (1911), 171–254.

TIMONEDA, JUAN. [*Cancionero llamado Sarao de amor*]. Valencia: Juan Navarro, 1561. This unique copy is in the National Library, Madrid: Raros 3857.

———. *El sobremesa y alivio de caminantes* (Valencia, 1569). Facsimile ed.; Madrid: Imprenta Alemana, 1917. Includes *Memoria hispanea*, *Memoria valentina*, and *Memoria poética*.

———. *Timón de tratantes*. Rev. ed.; Valencia: Pedro de Huete, 1575. The National Library, Madrid, catalogues this book as Raros 12880.

———. *Cancionero llamado Villete de amor*. Facsimile ed.; New York: De Vinne Press, 1903.

TORRE, LUCAS DE, ed. "Varias poesías de Juan Timoneda." *Boletín de la Real Academia Española*, 3 (1916), 564–70; 5 (1918), 506–10; 7 (1920), 86–95. Contains twelve chapbooks *(pliegos sueltos)*.

SECONDARY SOURCES

ALIN, JOSÉ MARÍA, ed. *El cancionero español de tipo tradicional*. Madrid: Taurus, 1968. An important study and anthology of the traditional-type refrain. Includes many examples from Timoneda.

ALMELA Y VIVES, FRANCISCO. *Valencia y su reino*. Valencia: Ediciones Mariola, 1965. Perhaps the best one-volume account of things Valencian. The Bibliography, pp. 685–718, is especially valuable.

ARÓSTEGUI, MARÍA PILAR. "La dramaturgia de Juan Timoneda: Estado actual de la cuestión." *Boletín de la Biblioteca de Menéndez Pelayo*, 48 (1972), 201–30. A useful summary of previous scholarship.

ARRÓNIZ, OTHÓN. *La influencia italiana en el nacimiento de la comedia española*. Madrid: Gredos, 1969. Illuminates Timoneda's role in transmitting Italian influence during the formative period of the Spanish *comedia*.

CHILDERS, J. WESLEY. *Motif-Index of the "Cuentos" of Juan Timoneda*. Bloomington: Indiana University, 1948. Classification and arrangement, based on Stith Thompson (see below), of the *Patrañuelo* and the two books of facetiae.

CRAWFORD, J. P. W. *Spanish Drama before Lope de Vega*. Rev. ed.; Philadelphia: University of Pennsylvania Press, 1937. Reprinted in 1967 with corrections and bibliographical supplement by Warren T. McCready. Valuable on Timoneda, his predecessors, and his contemporaries.

DELGADO BARNÉS, PILAR. "Contribución a la bibliografía de Juan de Timoneda." *Revista de Literatura*, 16 (1959), 24–56. Useful bibliography of editions, but must be used with caution.

EOFF, SHERMAN H. "The *Patrañuelo* of Juan de Timoneda: An Edition with

Introduction and Notes." Doctoral dissertation, University of Chicago, 1929. Especially valuable on the sources and analogues of the *patrañas*.

FROLDI, RINALDO. *Lope de Vega y la formación de la comedia. En torno a la tradición dramática valenciana y al primer teatro de Lope.* Salamanca and Madrid: Anaya, 1968. Points up the role of Timoneda and other Valencians in the development of the Lopean *comedia*.

GILLET, JOSEPH E. *Propalladia and Other Works of Bartolomé Torres Naharro*. 4 vols. Bryn Mawr and Philadelphia: University of Pennsylvania Press, 1943–61. Volumes 3 and 4—the latter completed by O. H. Green—are a mine of information on the language and literature of the sixteenth century.

GREEN, OTIS H. *Spain and the Western Tradition*. 4 vols. Madison: University of Wisconsin Press, 1963–66. Contains many pertinent discussions, e.g., courtly love, suicide, the Index, etc.

MARTÍ GRAJALES, FRANCISCO. *Ensayo de un diccionario biográfico y bibliográfico de los poetas que florecieron en el reino de Valencia hasta el año 1700.* Madrid: Tip. de la "Revista de Archivos, Bibliotecas y Museos," 1927. A fundamental work for the study of Timoneda's biography and bibliography.

MENÉNDEZ Y PELAYO, MARCELINO. *Orígenes de la novela*. Ed. Enrique Sánchez Reyes. 4 vols. Madrid and Santander: Consejo Superior de Investigaciones Científicas, 2nd ed. 1962. Volume 3 includes an important study of the *Patrañuelo* and the *Sobremesa*.

REGUEIRO, JOSÉ M. "Juan Timoneda y la tradición dramática española." Doctoral dissertation, University of Pennsylvania, 1972. For the abstract of this useful work, see *Dissertation Abstracts International-Humanities*, Vol. 33A, Nos. 10–12, 1973, pp. 6881A–6882A.

RODRÍGUEZ-MOÑINO, ANTONIO. *Diccionario bibliográfico de pliegos sueltos poéticos (siglo XVI)*. Madrid: Castalia, 1970. Includes full bibliographical data on Timoneda's chapbooks.

———. *Manual bibliográfico de cancioneros y romanceros (siglo XVI)*. 2 vols. Madrid: Castalia, 1973. Indispensable for the study of Timoneda's songbooks and ballad collections.

———. *Poesía y cancioneros (siglo XVI)*. Madrid: Real Academia Española, 1968. Includes an important study of Timoneda's songbooks.

ROMEU I FIGUERAS, JOSEP. *Joan Timoneda i la "Flor de enamorados," cançoner bilingüe: Un estudi i una aportació bibliogràfica.* Barcelona: Reial Acadèmia de Bones Lletres, 1972. An outstanding analysis of this celebrated *cancionero*.

ROTUNDA, D. P. *Motif-Index of the Italian Novella in Prose*. Bloomington: Indiana University, 1942. Very useful for the study of Italian sources and/or analogues of Timoneda's stories and anecdotes. Based on Stith Thompson (see below).

SANCHIS GUARNER, MANUEL. *La llengua dels valencians.* 4th ed. Valencia: L'Estel, 1972. On the history and present state of the Valencian variety of Catalan.

SERRANO Y MORALES, J. E. *Reseña histórica en forma de diccionario de las imprentas que han existido en Valencia desde la introducción del arte tipográfico en España hasta el año 1868.* Valencia: Imprenta de F. Domenech, 1898–99. A fundamental bio-bibliographical study.

SPERONI, CHARLES. *Wit and Wisdom of the Italian Renaissance.* Berkeley and Los Angeles: University of California Press, 1964. Fine study and anthology of the facetia in Italy. Includes many analogues and/or sources of Timoneda's anecdotes.

THOMPSON, STITH. *Motif-Index of Folk-Literature.* Rev. ed. 6 vols. Bloomington: Indiana University Press, 1955–58. Indispensable analysis of folktales. For current research on the folktale, consult *Fabula,* the Journal of Folktale Studies, published in Berlin from 1957 to date.

## ADDENDUM

While the present study was in press, the following noteworthy book appeared:

*Pliegos poéticos españoles de la Biblioteca Nacional de Viena.* Edición en facsímile precedida de un estudio por María Cruz García de Enterría. Madrid: Joyas Bibliográficas, 1975. This limited edition in two parts includes the facsimiles, as well as short studies, of Timoneda's *Dechado de colores, Enredo de amor, Guisadillo de amor,* and *El truhanesco.*

# Index

(Where no author is indicated, a work is either anonymous or by Timoneda.)